Matt is the real deal! His coaching and three-pillar system has helped me tremendously over the years. His programs have given me the balance, strength and conditioning to perform at my best throughout my career while riding all around the world giving stunt shows and seminars. His personal development coaching has gotten me through some tough times, helping me become who I am today. You won't find a better high performance life coach anywhere!

Chris "Teach" McNeil, Champion Freestyle Motorcycle Athlete and Professional Rider for BMW Motorrad

I've known Matt and his family for years. His dedication to his profession is unmatched. He follows his heart and without a doubt is one of the best top-notch coaches on the planet. If you want to change your life, look no further. You just have to take the first step.

Jorge Verdias, Founder and CEO, GAD Detailing

Matt has been a real catalyst for change, always pushing me and empowering me to realize the potential within myself. This has truly been a gift. I am thankful that he has helped to open my eyes to the ... hole new reality for me.

Nick Melvin, Entrepreneur

... unbelievable passion for life and what he helps accomplish for clients are his greatest attributes. You won't find anyone more driven to help you succeed.

Lance Dellogono, Silver Line Investments

10 STEPS TO CHANGING YOUR REALITY

MATT TAMAS

NEW YORK

LONDON • NASHVILLE • MELBOURNE • VANCOUVER

QUANTUM SUCCESS

Published in New York, New York, by Morgan James Publishing. Morgan James is a trademark of Morgan James, LLC.
www.MorganJamesPublishing.com

The Morgan James Speakers Group can bring authors to your live event. For more information or to book an event visit The Morgan James Speakers Group at
www.TheMorganJamesSpeakersGroup.com.

ISBN 978-1-68350-603-4 paperback
ISBN 978-1-68350-604-1 eBook
Library of Congress Control Number: 2017908337

Cover & Interior Design by:
Megan Whitney
Creative Ninja Designs
megan@creativeninjadesigns.com

CONTENTS

FOREWORD

by Chris "Teach" McNeil

I remember the day like it was yesterday: 22 years old, being badly bloodied and rushed to the ER from a motorcycle stunt gone wrong. Many of my friends and family shook their head in knowing disapproval, because motorcycles are dangerous and schoolteachers definitely shouldn't be doing tricks. My lifelong best friend, Matt Tamas, was there too, telling me in his matter of fact way how much of an idiot I was for not being properly geared up; but he was also encouraging me to get back out there and to think beyond just a wheelie in a parking lot – and he had some physical training that he thought could help me get there.

This was early in my career, before I had a career, and even before there was much of an opportunity to even make a career as a stunt rider; and at that time Matt's personal focus was on physical health and improvement, which helped me get to where I physically needed to be to achieve my goals. But the real difference maker was when Matt began developing and showing me the early stages of his high performance personal development mindset program, which is now the book you're reading, *Quantum Success*.

At first, I was highly skeptical, especially because it was just Matt, my best friend, and he was a normal dude like myself, so what could he know that I didn't? But as time went on, his excitement only grew, and I could see a physical difference in the way he carried himself and how it affected those around him, myself included. Fast forward 10 years, through the struggles and triumphs, the failures and successes, the disappointment and elation, and not only am I one of the first success stories of *Quantum Success* in my everyday personal life, I am now a seasoned, former World Stunt Riding Champion who successfully runs a demo program as a BMW Motorrad factory rider.

I tell the condensed version of that story to not only try to convey to you how life changing Matt's program can be, but to show you an example of one more real person who is living it every single day, right alongside of Matt. In today's world, we are inundated with a constant stream of get-rich-quick schemes and easy fixes. There is too much information, and it can seem impossible to cut through that mess and discern the good from the bad, the scam from the authentic. And that's the thing, Matt is as authentic as they come, living his own words, day in and day out; and he has been for as long as I've known him, nearly 40 years!

Matt's book, *Quantum Success,* exudes his down-to-earth, straightforward style and is filled with real-world examples that demonstrate the veracity of the principles of his program.

Matt's ability to practically apply theory to common every day interactions resonates with readers. He will show you how to take responsibility for your reality and grasp the power of your mindset so that you can understand how to most effectively change it. He will help you change the lens in which you view the world; and in true Tamas fashion, talk is never good enough — he will drive you to action through exercises in each chapter designed to help you put this new understanding into daily practice.

Quantum Success — applicable immediately, any walk of life, no skills necessary. Matt can help you change your course.

Chris 'Teach' McNeil

World Stunt Riding Champion and BMW Factory Rider

INTRODUCTION

Have you ever hit a crossroads in your life? One pivotal moment when the next decision you had to make would change your life forever?

I remember sitting yoga style on the floor of my cold, dark bedroom one night eleven years ago. I was alone, my head buried in my hands, sobbing uncontrollably. I remember saying to myself, *This is it.*

That's when I was faced with my moment.

I was going through a difficult divorce. My son's future was in danger because I didn't have full custody. I had filed bankruptcy. I had lost my house, which was being auctioned off the next day. And, on top of it all, I was dealing with non-stop harassment.

As I sat there, I contemplated for the first time in my life what it would be like if I just gave up, if I gave in, if I shut down my business and decided just to bag groceries for the rest of my life – if I discarded my vision and dreams. With everything going on, things were just too hard. What if I took the easy way out?

That was my moment. But these thoughts were at war with everything my family stood for. In my family, quitting was never an option. You didn't quit – ever. As I sat there struggling, I thought about my dad and his struggles. How he escaped Hungary back in 1956 in the middle of the night when he was just seven years old; how he and his family boarded a train to Luxembourg and from there were taken by horse and buggy along the long river that separated Hungary and Austria.

They were in dire trouble. To survive, it was imperative that they cross one of the bridges and reach the other side of the river. They approached the bridges one by one, but the Russian army was always there before them. Each bridge they approached was blown up before they could get there.

Only the last bridge was still intact. My dad's family, along with some other families they were travelling with, asked a Hungarian soldier with an army truck if he would take them over it. They paid him all the money they could. The families hid in the back of the truck bed so they wouldn't be seen.

At the last Russian checkpoint before the bridge, the driver was pulled over. The Russian soldiers ordered him to get out of the truck. They decided to check the back.

The soldiers ordered the driver to shut off the vehicle first. He got back in the truck to kill the engine. Then he saved them all – he threw the truck in drive.

The Russian guards immediately began firing their weapons at the Hungarian. If they'd shot out the truck's tires, it would all have been over. But they failed! The families made it to the last bridge before it was blown up and were able to cross into Austria to safety.

The rest is history. My dad came to America. He couldn't speak English, so he had to learn another language, and he worked his tail off. He served in the army in the Vietnam War for eighteen months and built two welding businesses. He has been married to my mom for forty-one years, brought up four children, and now has eight grandchildren. My dad could have given up at so many points, but he didn't, even though the odds were stacked up against him. In the beginning, he had no money, no English, nothing!

After everything he went through, how could I not fight? I made the decision right there and then. If I took the alternative path, the easy way out, the darkness would prevail. I would be giving up not just on my life, but my son's life. There was no way I was going to do that.

In that moment, I decided that there was something bigger at stake. It was my son's safety. It was our future. It was my vision of being successful and providing not only for my son but the future family I envisioned.

Everything seemed to be going against me, but, now, when I look back, it was all going perfectly. It was going the way it needed to go to get me where I am.

Soon after making the decision to keep fighting, I met my soul mate. Over the next two years, I fought for and won sole physical and legal custody of my son. In the past ten years with Krissy, we have had two more beautiful children, built two successful companies, and I have authored three books.

If I had chosen the easier path, the path of least resistance, nothing in my present life would be here. My family wouldn't exist, nor would anything that we have accomplished.

I learned a valuable lesson that cold, dark night, sobbing alone in the house I was about to lose. Even in the darkest of times, you can look within yourself and find a spark – a reason to prevail, to achieve everything you deserve, everything you envision. Decisions can be driven by desperation or inspiration. But regardless of what has gone before, success starts with a decision.

What was your moment? The moment you realized everything rested on your next decision. Is this it?

DEFINING SUCCESS

The Merriam-Webster dictionary definition of "success" is: *The attainment of wealth, favor, or eminence.* When most people judge whether someone is successful or not, they look at their position, their income and their material possessions: Are they someone's boss? Is their salary six figures? Do they have a big house? Do they have a flashy car? Being successful is often equated to vast amounts of riches, hitting the top of a corporate ladder, or standing at the head of an entrepreneurial empire.

It's important to recognize, though, that someone's idea of success is highly personal. In reality, success means different things to different people. It really doesn't matter what position you've reached or what possessions you have – what matters is that you have achieved happiness, fulfillment, abundance, whatever those terms mean to you.

To me, success is in living my dreams – even those that might seem impossible to other people. In my role as a personal safety instructor, it is in teaching someone the tools they need to prevail against violence – tools that can save their life. As an entrepreneur, it's in building a far-reaching business and creating a paradigm shift in my industry, connecting a network of like-minded souls and helping billions of people. As a husband and father, it's in nurturing my family and, in partnership with my wife, providing my children with a loving home where they can learn how to shape their own dreams. Overall, it's about being inspired to work towards something bigger than myself. Motivation fades over time. Being *inspired* is a flame deep down inside your core being that will never burn out.

Things may be different for you. We likely have different dreams. What's important is that, in order to go on to achieve the life you want, you define what success means *to you*. Maybe it *does* have a dollar amount – that's fine. Maybe it is reaching a certain position, or being able to live in a certain location, obtaining the freedom to create art, or having the time to appreciate it.

Whatever it is, no dream is impossible. Everything is possible. Forget about looking at everyone else, judging how successful they are, and assessing how successful you are in relation to them. Everyone can be successful. Success is not a finite resource. Life holds infinite possibilities.

HOMEOSTASIS

So why, if everything is possible, doesn't everyone have exactly what they want? Why do people say, *I can't*, or *Not me...*?

Often, people remain stuck in a state of inertia rather than taking the appropriate action to get them where they want to be. They exist in a state of homeostasis. Their dreams are only wishes; they don't believe in them, so they have no power.

People resist leaving the comfort zone because they don't like to take risks. But risk is a matter of perception – isn't the greater risk that you miss out on achieving everything you ever wanted?

The simple fact of the matter is that we are conditioned to think we don't like change. Generally, we only look to get a new job when we lose the old one or when we stop enjoying it; we only look to work on weight loss, fitness and nutrition once we become overweight, unfit and have health problems; we often only decide to consider our personal safety once something has already happened to us or someone close to home.

To make a change is to make an effort. The path of least resistance, of least stress and discomfort, is to do nothing – to remain in suspended animation. The problem with this, though, is that you don't get anywhere.

If you want things to be different – to be better – you have to make a decision. The question is, what drives someone to make a decision? As I've mentioned, it can be desperation or inspiration – but *you* get to choose. If you want more, if you want to grasp that elusive essence of success, then it's time to choose something bigger.

THE QUANTUM SOLUTION

We are constantly learning more about the nature of the world and the nature of our selves. We've come to an ever-increasing understanding that everything is energy. Quantum physics, which studies life at the smallest, subatomic level, tells us we exist in a field of infinite possibilities.

What does this mean for our everyday lives, for our attainment of success, however we define it? Reality is fluid. Everything is energy, including our very thoughts. Intangible thoughts have the ability to affect the "physical" world – reality as we perceive it. Thoughts – ideas – become things. As Napoleon Hill says in *Think and Grow Rich*, "The imagination is literally the workshop wherein are fashioned all plans created by man." Nothing is created or achieved that is not first an idea. If we shape our idea of success, it follows that we can achieve it.

Whatever you think about the ultimate or intricate nature of things, you can train your mind to take control and create your very reality. And here's the amazing part: If you don't believe it's possible, you can even retrain your mind to believe that it is. And once you believe it's possible, so it becomes – once you take action. It's being proved experientially over and over again. It's seeping into the mainstream in films and books such as Rhonda Byrne's *The Secret.* Soon, it will be irrefutable. Whether you think life is a simulation or a game, you can make the rules. All it takes is acting on your ideas to bring your desires to life. As Wallace Wattles says in *The Science of Getting Rich*, 'By thought, the thing you want is brought to you; by action, you receive it.'

All it takes is a decision threaded with action – a decision to be at cause rather than effect. Wake up in the morning and, rather than face your reality, *create* it yourself. When you approach life this way, it is just as easy to be successful as it is to be unsuccessful. This book will show you *how* to approach life this way and make your reality everything you dream.

WHO IS THIS BOOK FOR?

I wrote my previous book on self-protection, *Reinvent Your Personal Safety*, for my daughters, the women closest to me, and women all over the world. My aim was to cause a paradigm shift in personal safety. Every step of the way, I had my daughters in mind. This book is different. That pivotal decision all those years ago was sparked by my son, Peter. This book is for all my children, and especially for the son I fought so hard to get back. It's my duty as their father and role model to give them the tools, tactics and strategies to succeed in life, regardless of how well they do in school or what others try telling them. I want this book to be a handbook that any of my children can pick up when they're ready and learn from and follow.

This book is for them, but it's also for you. It is really for anyone who wants to achieve his or her dreams and is willing to put in the hard work to do it. It is a template for success – a complete guide to a life of abundance.

It doesn't matter what background you have – where you come from, where your family came from. It doesn't matter what level of education you've had. Some of the most successful people in the world have reached the heights they have without having had an advanced, formal education.

Everyone's been conditioned in some way, shape or form. Everyone can put the guidance in this book into practice and break the mold. The guidance is given in such a way that it can be applied practically to a reader's life, and the reader can tailor it to their individual circumstances and desires.

WHO IS THIS BOOK BY?

Who am I and why should you listen to me? I'm no self-help "guru" and I'm not selling you a magic pill; I'm just a high performance person who has taken massive action and has learned how to get everything he's ever wanted. This isn't the kind of thing you keep to yourself! There's more than enough success to go around.

My career started in the field of strength and conditioning nearly twenty years ago. After becoming a certified strength and conditioning specialist, I turned my focus on the field of self-protection. I completed multiple personal safety certifications under coach Tony Torres, who developed the Functional Edge System of self-protection, while studying the best teaching principles and training programs around the world with a multitude of instructors. I incorporated everything I learned into my own consulting business and have been coaching people in personal safety ever since, from lawyers, athletes and entrepreneurs to CEOs and moms.

The research and training didn't stop there, with my passion for teaching people the best way to protect themselves only becoming deeper, alongside my desire for self-improvement. I undertook mentorships with leadership expert Scott Mann, a retired Green Beret, as well as executive coach Peter Sage, a renowned public speaker and expert in personal development. In order to further explore my potential specifically business potential, I have also mentored and continue to mentor under multi-billionaire Errol Abramson, who has started, bought and turned around over forty-four companies, taking four of them over the annual billion dollar mark.

What I have found in the course of my work is that self-protection has come to mean much more to me than the ability to prevail against physical violence – and that's where this book has come from. Protecting your Self isn't only about fending off violent forces – it's about achieving your full potential, physically, mentally and emotionally. These aspects are all tied together. There are three pillars to my holistic concept of self-protection: personal safety; personal development; and health and wellness. This book obviously concentrates on the second of these, but in my mind, they are all bound together.

I founded ReWiredAcademy.com to bring together like-minded men who want to lead a life of impact, wealth and freedom; to give them the tools and support they need to live the life they were meant to live.

I've been leading from the trenches for the last eighteen years, coaching strength and conditioning, personal development and personal safety. And every day, I've been practicing the principles I'm about to describe to you – I've been putting into action everything you are about to read.

Let me be clear. I am no different from you. We are truly all one; we are all connected. But I am not here to push my views, especially my view of the world, onto you. I am just here to let you know the tools, tactics and strategies that have helped me in my own life because I know that they can help you in yours. This is the book I wish I'd been handed when I was younger – it's a cheat sheet, putting together everything I have learned that has got me where I am. Though I don't regret the journey it's taken me to get here – and it's served its purpose teaching me everything I know – I want to give you a head start.

Take what you can from it and create your reality from what you find useful. All I can promise you is that you *can* change your life and achieve your wildest dreams. The guidance in this book will help show you how.

10 STEPS TO CHANGING YOUR REALITY

The principles I present here are a template to success. They make up a holistic approach to personal development that allows you to form your own Quantum Success Plan. There are ten key elements to apply:

1. **Take responsibility** – It has to start with you. Happiness isn't caused by external events; *you* are the one who can make yourself happy and successful. In this step, we'll look at being selfish; bearing your crosses; and becoming accountable.

2. **Access your vision** – It's important to dream big. You need to visualize success and "live as if when without." In this step, we'll identify the spark that drives your vision; give you permission to dream; and explore the elements of effective visualization.

3. **Trust your gut** – Your sixth sense is the most important of all the senses. In this step, we'll talk about what your intuition is; what listening to your intuition feels like; and the alignment of heart and mind.

4. **Design your environment** – When you let go of toxicity and control whom and what surrounds you, in turn, you control who you are. In this step, we'll look at the three elements of your environment: places, people and media, and address your choices when it comes to controlling each area.

5. **Look after yourself** – This is about building a better you, physically as well as mentally. In this step, we'll go through the basics of three integral principles of self-care: nutrition, exercise and recovery.

6. **Break down your barriers** – Reprogramming your mind is not only possible but also revolutionary when it comes to achieving your dreams. In this step, we'll look at limiting beliefs and how to overcome them; and the best way to practice positive affirmations.

7. **Reframe failure** – Put simply, failure is education. It is success disguised. In this step, we'll examine the nature of failure; how to look at things from a different perspective; and the way to turn failure into success.

8. **Invest in yourself** – You truly get out what you put in. Investment – in terms of time, energy and/or money – is the personification of your commitment. In this step, we'll identify your most valuable asset; look at the benefits of mentorship; and consider how to find the right mentor.

9. **Communicate with others** – This is about the rewards of empathy and the principle of reciprocity. In this step, we'll look at the importance of conversation; ways in which we can help one another; and how to engage in active listening.

10. **Create your reality** – When you put everything together, take appropriate action and make that leap of faith, this is when you truly create your own reality. In this step, we'll recognize our outer world as a reflection of our inner world; and see how, with self-belief, you can mold yourself and your life into everything you desire them to be. You forge the key to your success.

Your beliefs need to be aligned with the decisions you make and the actions you take or you'll end up in conflict. This is something you'll visit time and time again throughout the steps in this book – there needs to be consistency in the emotional, mental and physical engagement with the principles I'm going to teach you. This is the foundation for success.

As we go through these principles, you'll find examples and exercises to help you engage with the material. At the end of the day, it's not about theory; it's about performance. I'm going to show you how you can perform to your utmost potential and truly change your life. It's not that anything is possible. Everything is possible.

1 TAKE RESPONSIBILITY

There's a saying in personal security: "You Are It." When it comes to personal safety, one of the most important lessons you can learn is to take responsibility for yourself.

This is equally the case when it comes to your personal development. You are the first responder to any situation that arises. You can't rely on anyone else to live your life for you. If you let others create your reality, then you live by their rules, their definitions. You live by their leave. At the end of the day, while you can take the advice of others and follow their guidance, *you* are the one who makes the decision, whether that is to accept the status quo or challenge it. You are the star in your own movie. Don't focus on other people's lives – in most people's lives, you're just an extra. This is *your* show.

This first step is one of the most important. This is your declaration of accountability. This is where you decide to live at cause rather than effect, and be the captain of your own ship. You are the only thing that you can control; but when you take control of your thoughts and your actions, you control your reality.

When things happen, it is not down to them that you are happy or sad. You are the one who attaches emotions to events and to material possessions. Happiness isn't caused by external events; *you* are the only one who can make yourself happy and successful.

You can see this playing out around you all the time. Think of the most negative person you know. Imagine their car breaks down and they have to walk or get public transport to work. The first thing they do is moan about it, ranting, *Why me? Everything bad always happens to me.* They will whine about it all day, blaming it for being late to work and for things that then go wrong at work. They let the negative emotions take over, deciding the universe has it in for them.

Meanwhile, picture the most positive person you know. They're unlikely to have the same reaction to the same event. They take a different perspective when things go wrong. They might say, *Things like this happen. Much worse things have already happened to other people today. I'm grateful for the reminder.* They probably enjoy the walk or end up having a nice chat with someone on the bus. They don't hold the external event responsible for the rest of their day. They understand that *they* control their emotions. They own their reality.

In short, you have to own your reality before you can change it.

PERMISSION TO PUT YOURSELF FIRST

The first thing I'm going to ask you to do is be selfish.

Let me clarify: When I tell you to be selfish, I'm talking about taking care of *you* first. It's only by taking care of yourself that you can help others.

Just think about when you are on a flight and the flight attendants take you through the safety demonstration. If there is a loss in cabin pressure, air masks will drop down in front of you. And what do the flight attendants always say? They tell you to put the mask over your own face *first*. They say that by taking care of yourself first, you'll be better able to help your loved ones next.

But it seems like the more selfish act, right? Why can't you just slip the mask over the child beside you first – the more "unselfish" thing to do? Isn't that normally what we do – put the children first?

The thing is, hypoxia (oxygen deprivation) can set in incredibly rapidly. It may come with warning signs: shortness of breath, dizziness, blurry vision and mental confusion. But at higher altitudes, depressurization and unconsciousness can occur within a few seconds. You can't help anyone else if you pass out in the process. It's more efficient to take care of your needs first so you can assist children and other passengers with your full faculties intact, however selfish the act of saving yourself first might seem.

Take an example in a broader context. Imagine someone running around here, there and everywhere, so focused on their loved ones and helping everyone else that they lose sight of taking care of themselves in the process.

They wake up early in the morning in order to get the kids ready and get them off to school. They make sure that the kids have breakfast, but they don't have time to grab something themselves. Then they hit traffic and have to get themselves to work. Work is busy, so they don't grab more than some coffee and, later, takeout to eat at their desk. They work late, then hit traffic, then make it home. Their partner's picked up the kids and sorted them out with dinner, but the kids still need help with their homework. Then a colleague calls, needing a favor or an ear to bend, and they don't have the heart to say they don't have time to do what's asked of them. They don't eat till late, then only get to watch a little television before bed and the whole cycle starts again.

They make unhealthy food choices, don't make time for exercise, become overweight, don't make time for relaxation (that would be selfish), and the list goes on... Life can spiral out of control. Focusing on everything and everyone except yourself, it's easy to neglect your diet and exercise, sacrifice your sleep and lose touch with your friends and personal interests. You might consider yourself the most selfless person around, but what do you think happens next?

You become stressed. And stress can cause a variety of problems, internal and external, including physical ailments and chronic illness. You turn into the one who needs help, and your ability to help others is forfeited.

Even though you have spent all this time refusing to be selfish, it backfires, because then you require others to be selfless in order to look after you. And you're in no position to look after them in return.

Being selfish in this context is one of the most important things you can do, not just for your own health and wellbeing but also that of others.

In my previous book, I said it's the same thing when it comes to your personal safety, and I'm going to say it again: It's the same thing when it comes to your personal development.

If you go day by day, ignoring opportunities and not investing the time in improving your life because, subconsciously, you think focusing that time and energy on yourself would be selfish, then you have to think again. Do you want the others around you, especially your loved ones, to be happy and healthy? Then be happy and healthy yourself – and see how it rubs off on them! Do you want others around you to achieve their dreams? Then achieve your own – show them it's possible, that everything is possible. Inspire change by first changing yourself.

Put yourself first, even if the idea seems selfish. Put the mask on yourself before doing anything else. You are a VIP – there is nothing wrong with admitting your worth to yourself. Embracing being selfish is the same as rejecting feeling guilty. Feeling guilty for investing in yourself and achieving for yourself gains you nothing. And once you *have*, then you can share. I'll revisit this principle of reciprocity later in the book. The thing to grasp now is that part of preparation for achieving your dreams is accepting that you need to take care of yourself first. It doesn't take that much time and, with minimal investment, you get a huge reward. You protect what's most valuable – you!

BEAR YOUR CROSSES

One key point to remember throughout all of this is never to wish you could be someone else.

We are all given a deck of cards specific to us. Some aspects of our lives will be great, some not so great. This is the game of life; expect both! You have to experience the lows to truly appreciate the highs in your life.

We are all equal. We all have crosses to bear; they just appear in many different sizes, shapes and colors. Some people deal with abuse, some deal with health issues, some deal with losing a close friend or close relative, some have mental problems or physical ailments, some deal with divorce, some deal with drug and alcohol problems ... the list goes on and on.

The point I am trying to make is that the grass is sometimes going to appear greener. But you don't really know someone until you walk a mile in their shoes, so stop and really think when you find yourself wishing you had someone else's life. Chances are, you don't know the crosses that they have to bear. Chances are, you're better off playing with the deck of cards you've been dealt. Your circumstances are what have formed the person you are today and made you unique.

That's what I meant in the introduction when I told my story and said that, looking back, things were going perfectly.

Eleven years ago, things looked bleak. I was suffering. So much so, I contemplated giving up. Facing divorce, bankruptcy, child custody battles and harassment – these were my crosses to bear. But they've brought me where I am. They've made possible everything that's come to happen since.

You might think I would wish I hadn't married my first wife. But without that marriage, I would not have my son. If I hadn't come through that eight-month marriage, I might not have met my current wife of ten years. You might think I would wish never to have experienced bankruptcy. But without that experience, I might not appreciate the abundance I've gone on to create. My experience of divorce and child custody battles has made me never take a moment of my happy marriage and life with my family for granted. I appreciate everything I have. Finally, you might think I would wish never to have gone through years of harassment. But if so – you're still not getting it. That experience has given me empathy for others who undergo the same kind of abuse. It makes me a better personal safety coach because I understand the mental, emotional and physical aspects of violence that, sadly, people have to contend with in this world. I regret nothing.

That's not to say I want to relive negative experiences and that's not to say that you should just accept it if things are bad. I'm saying the opposite. You can accept negative experiences are a part of life, but you can still fight to turn your life around and make it a better one. The trick is not to waste time and energy bemoaning what's going wrong – that will only attract more wrong. The trick is to drive time and energy into pursuing what's right – guess what that attracts?

You might look at someone's life and think you want to be him or her, but you wouldn't necessarily want to go through everything they've been through. You can only really know yourself and your own life. That's what you control. You shouldn't focus on comparisons and competition. When I was faced with my moment, I thought back to what my dad had been through and I thought about what I wanted for my son – that's what drove me forward. If I had wasted time envying other people their picture-perfect lives, it would have been a complete misdirection of the energy I found within myself to keep fighting.

Expect great times and bad times. Life is Yin and Yang. It's in balance, just like nature. You must go with the flow of life. Nothing in nature is a straight line. Life doesn't operate that way. It's like a river. You just have to go with the flow and navigate yourself in that flow, trusting that the bends in the river are the quickest path to where you're going.

So bear your crosses. If something happens in the outer world, can you change it? No, it's already happened! The only thing you can do is accept it, respond appropriately and focus on the positive in your inner world – your metaphysical world. That is what will bring more positive developments to your external reality.

BECOME ACCOUNTABLE

At the end of his book *Think and Grow Rich*, Napoleon Hill presents a list of alibis. There are lots and lots of them and they all begin: *IF* ...

IF I had money...

IF I had a good education...

IF conditions around me were only different...

IF I didn't have so many worries...

IF luck were not against me...

These are excuses! These alibis shift the blame for not achieving success to factors outside you. They comfort you as you continue to exist in a state of homeostasis, perceiving yourself as trapped in the status quo. But this is a prison you yourself have created – it only exists in your mind!

Hill quotes Elbert Hubbard: "It has always been a mystery to me why people spend so much time deliberately fooling themselves by creating alibis to cover their weaknesses. If used differently, this same time would be sufficient to cure the weakness, then no alibis would be needed."

Becoming accountable is about recognizing that this choice is in your hands – again, it is in your mind! The fact that you have picked up this book means that you want to make a change. You have given yourself permission to think greater than your current circumstances. This very act means that greatness is within your reach.

People aren't always conscious that their first instinct is to deny or shift responsibility. But there's nothing stopping *you* from being conscious of it, and choosing to take responsibility for what unfolds.

Buy yourself a notebook or open a new document on your computer and make yourself a journal. I call mine my "Quantum Success Journal" because that's what it's all about – performing to the best of my potential each and every day. It doesn't matter when or where you write your journal or even how much you write – what matters is that it becomes a habit. (There'll be more in this book on how to break bad habits and form new ones later!)

I'm going to keep coming back to this journal each chapter and ask you to record your response to the material in this book as well as perform some of the exercises. Writing down your intentions is very important. It gives them power. As well as writing about things that happen, you're also going to write about things that are going to happen – and commit to them. You'll be amazed at what begins to happen when you do. Choices and opportunities will come out of leftfield, giving you the chance to move towards what you really want – grab them and keep going!

For this first exercise, write about what happened today and write about your commitment to read this book. Mention the subject of the first chapter – taking responsibility, and do the following:

- Give yourself permission to put yourself first! Go on, write down your intention to be more selfish – I dare you. It doesn't matter what anyone else thinks, but if that's the kind of thing that holds you back right now, understand that this journal is solely for you. It is completely private. You don't have to share it with anyone unless you want to. It is for you. So tell yourself what you're going to do – tell yourself you're going to take care of yourself first.
- If the idea of bearing your crosses resonated with you, I want you to do something further. Write down your crosses. What are the circumstances in your past or in your present that suck energy out of you – that bring you down? I don't want you to dwell on these things, but I want you to accept them. Write them down. Then write down ten good things next to each

that come out of them, just as I described for mine. Even if your cross is in the present, write as though it is in the past and as though you are experiencing the benefit now. In your inner world, you *can* experience that benefit now – don't worry, your external world will catch up. For example: *I filed bankruptcy. I had nothing ... BUT now I have abundance, I appreciate it all the more. This is part of my story now. It inspires others who lose everything when they see that I overcame this and now have everything I could ever want.*

- Lastly, record your declaration of accountability. Ignore any alibis that try to take possession of your mind – you're not going to feed them energy. You're going to play with the deck of cards you've been dealt and you're still going to win. Simply write the words: *I take responsibility for my reality.*

2 ACCESS YOUR VISION

When I talk about your "vision," what am I actually talking about? Your vision is generally regarded as your sight – your ability to see. In this context, I'm talking about your ability to see into the future.

For this, you use your imagination rather than your eyes, but the point I'm going to keep returning to in this book is that this experience is equally as "real" as anything you might focus on in the external world. And here's the kicker – you can form in the external world what you are able to see in your inner world. You just have to believe it's possible and form the most detailed, vivid imagining that you can.

I'm going to mention a couple of things up front here. The first is the difference between having a vision and setting goals. There are many proponents of goal setting, and breaking large tasks down into manageable to-do lists helps lots of people get things done incrementally. However, this isn't what I'm talking about. Setting goals is something I've tried myself, but it's been nowhere near as effective for getting me where I am as painting an "impossible" dream and holding it in my mind, feeling it through my body and focusing on it with all my intent.

The second thing I want to address is a common question that arises: What if my vision changes? Is my vision allowed to change? The answer is a resounding yes! As I said before, life doesn't move in a straight line. Reality is fluid. Your vision is allowed to evolve as you evolve, and you may find that the universe responds to you in mysterious ways. Focused on one possible future, opportunities and developments may arise that take you in a different direction if you so choose – to a new vision you didn't even know was possible until events unfolded.

I'm thinking of my own path here – I set out to become a strength and conditioning coach, working with pro athletes, but the further I went on my journey, the more I found different things popping up out of leftfield – my vision grew, my horizon expanded, and things that hadn't even crossed my mind in the beginning became a possibility. If I felt like pursuing them, I did, and watched them become a reality.

Often, in business, what you start out thinking will make you successful doesn't end up being *it*. It's amazing what comes up when you start seriously pursuing a dream.

FIND YOUR SPARK

Before you jump into painting your vision of the future, I want you to really think about why you are doing this. You need to know *why* because this will keep you going. This is your motivation, your inspiration, your spark. This is what ignites the jet fuel and lights a fire under you. This is what makes everything worthwhile.

This cropped up in the introduction, in my story, and this burning question will continue to crop up whenever anything becomes an effort, or takes up your time, or demands your energy, especially when things are hard, and you perceive they're not going your way. You'll need to stop, pause and think: *Why am I doing this? What is the point?*

For me, it was the thought of my son – what I wanted for him – primarily his safety, but then the possibility of a limitless future. When things were at their toughest, he was the spark that kept me fighting. I would think about why I was doing this – I wanted to be a role model for him. I wanted to achieve my dreams to prove that it was possible, so that he would have no problem ever believing that he could achieve his own.

Before we go any further, I want you to dedicate some serious thought to this. It might not take much digging at all to find your underlying motivation, but the more you think about it, the more it will become entrenched in your brain, ready to give you a kick of inspiration and motivation whenever you need it most.

These are the considerations when you are trying to identify your spark:

1. It must be personal.

2. It will be something or someone you are passionate about.

3. It has to be important to you NOW – something in the present, not something from the past.

4. It is what makes you tick. Deep down, it makes you who you are.

5. It is a trigger. The thought of losing it is what will get you fired up enough to fight for your vision.

6. It isn't logical; it's emotional – something that rips you at your core, deep in your heart and soul.

You need to take some time to uncover this part of yourself. It might be a very simple answer, but, again, you need to really think about it and engage your emotions at the same time. When the going gets tough, you want your brain to be programmed to immediately spark your resistance.

PERMISSION TO DREAM

Now comes the fun part. I want you to give yourself permission to dream. No dream is impossible, so dream big! The very fact that you have imagined it means that it is a possibility in the field of infinite possibilities. Napoleon Hill went so far as to clip the word "impossible" out of his dictionary.

Make your vision so crazy and out there that people think you're NUTS. If you aim for the moon, even if you "only" get half way, you will still hit the stars.

I always think of this story I was told. Two guys were at a party for New Year's and they both decided to write out what they wanted to accomplish by the following year's party. They put what they'd written inside an envelope and sealed it. The following year, the first guy opened up the envelope and took out his piece of paper excitedly. He told his friend that he hit his goal of making 100K. His friend took out his piece of paper and just looked at it. "Did you do it?" the first guy asked. "No," his friend replied. He only hit fifty per cent of what was written down. The thing is, the figure he'd written down was five million.

In *The Last Lecture*, Professor Randy Pausch talked about achieving his childhood dreams. Now these were pretty out there – as many of our childhood dreams tend to be! He wanted to experience zero gravity, author an article in the *World Book Encyclopedia*, be Captain Kirk, play in the NFL, be the guy who won giant stuffed animals at amusement parks, and be an Imagineer with Disney.

His route to going some, and in most cases all, the way to fulfilling these childhood dreams ties back to what I said before – your vision can change, and on the way to one dream, you can discover more than you ever imagined, even if you don't end up getting what you first aimed for. So it was that even though Dr. Pausch didn't actually play in the NFL, he says he "probably got more from that dream and not accomplishing it than from any of the dreams that [I] did accomplish." This was down to the fundamental life lessons he learned from his coaches.

Dr. Pausch truly taps into how you can give yourself permission to dream – even the kind of impossible dreams you have as a child – and go on to make them a reality. On that note, it really helps to approach life and success like a child. When you're a kid, you believe you can do anything. You haven't been conditioned (yet) to perceive that you "have a place" or that you shouldn't or can't do something. You are the center of the universe and you have limitless, effortless faith. That's what you need to find again now, even as an adult. Everything is possible.

Now here's another important point. Don't only give yourself permission to dream. Give yourself permission to *have*. So many people struggle with this concept. The idea of owning things that others don't or making their fortune can lead to them feeling consumed with guilt. This has been part of our conditioning, but it makes no sense! Only when you have can you share. And if you work hard and go the extra mile, why shouldn't you have everything you desire? You are not taking from others. There is more than enough to go around, and anyone can change their reality and go after what they want. Doing it for yourself proves to others that it's possible. It's not about having material possessions, but the meaning you attach to them.

Above all, you don't need to feel guilty for wanting something or making sure that you have it. For example, I've always dreamed of having a Ferrari or a McLaren. And I'm going to have one! I recently had a 2016 Torch Red Corvette Z06. I loved driving it – I enjoyed every minute of it. You wouldn't believe the conversations I had when I parked it from people coming over to talk to me.

That car was a touch point with people. It inspires an emotional connection that sparks conversations everywhere I went. Sometimes other people had their own personal stories about the Corvettes in their life and what they meant or mean to them. Other times, a young person is asking me how I got it because it's an inspiration to them. Now, I know that life is much more than having an amazing car, and I don't *need* it. I'm already happy within; I don't need to chase material items to give me happiness. If it were taken away tomorrow, I'd be living in just as much abundance. Abundance is all around us; just look at nature! The key here is that I have given myself permission to enjoy life to the fullest. And for me, personally, part of that means driving the car I love and sharing it with others.

Give yourself permission to dream, to have whatever you desire. You're human; it's okay! Give yourself permission to let go of guilt. The more you have, the more you can share. Let's contrast a different kind of dream; I want to tell you about another of mine. It was to visit a children's hospital in Boston on a holiday with my family and hand out gifts. There is no greater joy a human can experience on this planet than helping someone. Being able to visit and deliver joy to these children is simply amazing. It's a tradition I hope my children will continue when they're adults. For a while, it was a vision in my inner world – through taking appropriate action, I have transformed it into a reality in the physical world.

EFFECTIVE VISUALIZATION

So once you've found your spark and given yourself permission to dream, how do you put it into practice? The answer is effective visualization.

Think about how famous athletes visualize their success. They actually use mental training more than physical training because it allows them to train perfectly at all hours of the day. Take Dr. JoAnn Dahlkoetter's work with Olympic athletes as a sports psychologist and performance coach. She speaks of an Olympic speed skater she worked with and how visualization helped her to succeed. Dahlkoetter describes every step of the imagery the skater used, which incorporated all of her five senses into the experience: feeling her forefoot pushing off the track, hearing her skating splits, seeing herself surge ahead of her competition. Going through the elements of the race over and over again using mental training techniques meant she set a new American record at the Olympic Trials.

In the same way, Olympic skiers will go over the perfect run in their mind. They know every turn and how they will feel at each turn. Sometimes, on TV, they will actually show you the racer going through his/her mental training before the event – it's pretty cool to watch. They can see and feel themselves flying down the mountain as fast as they can possibly go and finishing a flawless race. They can tell you about the feel of the snow and the terrain at any point on the course.

Do you think that is the only time they are using visualization? Athletes imagine success twenty-four hours a day.

Practice really does make permanence. The important thing to note is that it has to be the right kind of visualization.

A lot of people speak about using visualization for success, but very few people really teach the different types of visualizing that people do on a day-to-day basis.

Most of the visualizing that people do is useless, because it is more like daydreaming. The mind wanders aimlessly with no direction or consistency; it's more of a distraction than anything productive. Daydreaming about something gets you nowhere; it just wastes valuable time.

Purposeful visualization is the form that most personal development gurus teach their students. However, in reality, it's very ineffective as well, and only slightly better than daydreaming. The only difference between daydreaming and purposeful visualization is that, with the latter, you may look at a picture on a wall, in your wallet or in your bathroom on a daily basis and focus on that, instead of just letting your mind wander with no visual to guide it.

To develop a truly helpful visualization technique, you need to do more.

The future that is created depends on where your attention goes. For visualization to truly create the outer world you envision, you must be fully engaged in your heart, mind and soul. That means your psychological, emotional and physical self all have to be one – completely aligned with each other.

The main point here is to really feel the emotions. If you don't feel the emotions within your body, then this process won't work. Your brain won't have anything to attach the experience to.

In Patti Dobrowolski's TEDx talk *draw your future*, she asks, "What dream or vision do you want to turn into reality?" She points out that the odds against making a change in your life are nine to one. Nine to one, she says, even if you're facing a life-threatening illness. These aren't great odds at all! But she goes on to present the solution to beating those odds and living the life you desire. She says, "It's right there in front of you, but in order to achieve it, you must first see it, then believe it, and then you must graciously ask and train your brain to help you execute your vision."

Talking about the power of a picture, she comments that a picture can create movements, unite nations, pull at your heart and fill you with a deep desire to do something. And it doesn't even have to be a complicated work of art. As Dobrowolski says, you don't have to be an artist. You can just simply draw your "current state" and then draw your "desired new reality," and you have an instant roadmap for change.

It can be stick figures; it can be sketchy. It really doesn't matter. What matters is that we're more easily able to remember something that's visual. That's why someone might suggest you look at pictures in a purposeful visualization exercise, as I mentioned. However, as Dubrowolski says, "You get the most power when you paint your own picture."

Then comes the important step – soaking in it, filling the picture with color, filling it with *emotion*, getting inside of it. You have to feel the emotions associated with having everything you want.

When you draw and dream, you engage the right side of your brain, the creative side. You silence the critical, analytical left side and release hormones like serotonin and oxytocin, which make you feel happy and motivated.

It comes down to drawing a picture compelling enough to spur you into action.

exercise: Access Your Vision

I'm going to ask you to complete an exercise in your journal, but first, I'm going to share something highly personal with you – an extract from my own Quantum Success Journal from a couple of years ago. This is how I act "as if when without" and really tap into my emotions when envisioning my success.

I love right now. I love knowing that I have no limits! I watch the Official Ferrari 488 Spider video and feel myself driving it! It is the most amazing experience in my life... Not only do I see myself driving a Ferrari 488 Spider but I feel the emotion, the excitement, the passion... I hear the sweetest sound on earth from the exhaust! It is amazing!

I see myself driving it to schools, giving talks and showing children and teens what is possible when you have your mind and soul in alignment. It truly is amazing. Words can't even describe how I am feeling right now in the moment. There aren't words in the English language, or any language for that matter, which can explain how I feel!

The universe is opening because I operate at a different level right now than I did yesterday. The past is gone, this is me, this is who I am! I am so wealthy in so many aspects of my life and it is amazing. My family, nature, people I meet, etc. ... there are an infinite number of things that I am grateful for and that are in abundance in my life right now at this moment.

I figured it out right now. I am going to finish my online program, buy my Ferrari and then go to schools to give motivational talks to kids to show them this is real! Reality is subject to influence so my life meets me halfway.

Better yet, I am going to be sponsored by Ferrari! They are going to give me a Ferrari 488 Spider so when I give motivational talks they are represented.

Telling someone your vision isn't always good because they are your dreams and visions. Conventional wisdom and average people are going to think you're nuts. But when people think you're nuts and off your rocker because of your vision for success, you KNOW YOU ARE ON THE RIGHT PATH!

The caption at the end of the Ferrari video is "create your ultimate drive." Now it's your turn. Open your notebook or your document and put your vision into words. Draw the pictures, as Patti Dobrowolski shows the audience in her TEDx talk. You can even make a mind movie: www.mindmovies.com.

Just make sure you engage your emotions. Seeing means believing. And, in this instance, believing means seeing.

3 TRUST YOUR GUT

Have you ever been faced with a difficult decision and had someone tell you to go with your gut? There might be a whole heap of pros and cons for each choice, and it's sometimes difficult to decide (using logic and reason alone) which way is the best way. When you tell someone to go with their gut, you're telling them to follow their heart. To ignore all the different arguments being drawn out by their busy brain and do what they *feel is right*.

There's a reason we encourage people to do this – our gut is on our side. It's the mouthpiece for our inner self, which obviously wants the best for us, and it's picked up on signs and signals so quickly that they haven't yet been articulated as messages in our conscious mind. We end up *just knowing* something without knowing the root cause.

Your intuition is your body's own personal security system, and has been hardwired into you through thousands of years of evolution. It is part of your subconscious. It is just something that knows without knowing how.

Intuition can be seen as non-rational, a concept in the realm of feeling rather than thinking. The psychologist Carl Jung defined it as "perception via the unconscious," and neuroscientific literature sees it as sitting predominantly in the non-dominant hemisphere of the brain. The conscious and unconscious minds are often likened to an iceberg, with the conscious mind being the part sitting above the water, dealing with our awareness and rational decisions, and the unconscious mind sitting below the water – the larger mass. This is where our unconscious beliefs reside, along with our memories, stored experiences and knowledge. And this is the part of us that guides our intuition.

You owe it to yourself to listen to that internal voice. It tells us when something is just not right. It talks to us by sending us feelings to experience, often in our gut.

LISTEN TO YOUR INTUITION

I started to hear that little voice in my gut way back in high school. I didn't understand it back then, but I had access to feelings that many people don't even acknowledge exist. This has led me to where I am today, because I have always listened to that little voice, no matter what road it has brought me down.

My mind always thought it was crazy, but my heart and soul knew where I was going. Your intuition is like a built-in navigation system, leading to where you are supposed to be in life at a specific moment.

The problem with this navigation system is that it doesn't always take you down the paved road that many others, including your logical brain, think it should.

Just think of the Kevin Costner movie, *Field of Dreams*. In the film, Costner's character started hearing a voice saying, 'If you build it, he will come.' What did he build? A baseball field, and he had to tear out rows of corn on his farm to do it.

This made no logical sense to him, his family or others in the community. But he followed his intuition, and extraordinary things started to happen as a result.

For me, I had a similar experience right after graduating high school. I was supposed to go to St Anselm's College in New Hampshire and then, mid-summer, my gut said NO. I called them and politely said that I would not be attending their school in September.

Instead, I did a 180-degree turn. I applied to the University of Wyoming, which was 2,600 miles from my little hometown in Massachusetts, and the rest is ... well, the rest is me!

It made no logical sense and more than a few people thought I was crazy. I actually didn't know too much about the school except that my uncle Rich had graduated from there – I just knew I had to go. Heck, I didn't even know how I would get to Laramie, where the university was. I ended up flying out to Colorado by myself, having never flown alone before. And back then wasn't like today. I had no cell phone, no Internet... If you moved far away from home, you truly felt it. With no family anywhere nearby, it was an odd choice to make to say the least.

But it was the best choice I could have made. That decision catapulted me to where I am right now. I grew from an extremely shy little eighteen-year-old boy into the man I would become during my four years there.

Yes, listening to your gut is important. It's part of acknowledging your self-worth to realize that *you* are worth listening to, whatever anyone else is saying.

Your intuition has been hardwired into you through thousands of years of evolution. It connects us all. You owe it to yourself to listen to that internal voice. As with my choice of college, it tells us when something is just not right. It sends us messages in several different ways, including uncertainty, hesitation, nagging feelings, curiosity, doubt, gut feelings, suspicion and, most powerful of all, fear.

If you get the feeling that something just isn't right, it probably isn't. Equally, if you get the feeling that you should go for something, even if it doesn't make logical sense, then you should! You need to learn to trust yourself. Trust your intuition.

ALIGN YOUR HEART AND MIND

Listening to your inner voice and following your heart isn't always a simple or easy thing to do, however. The reason for this is that our clever brains can often get in the way. We have been conditioned to look for the logical explanation in every situation, sometimes at the cost of ignoring the obvious. The more complex the solution we think, the better. At times, rational thinking even has a nasty habit of overriding common sense. We fight against our feelings rather than backing them up, when we would be so much more powerful and effective if we spent that energy aligning our heart and mind.

What does misalignment feel like? That's easy. If you're on the path that everyone else thinks you should be on, keeping your head down, listening to the logical arguments, but secretly yearning for a different life – you're living in opposition to yourself.

It is so easy to sabotage yourself and so hard to break free from the mold and go against conventional wisdom, especially if it is against the advice of people you love and respect. But sometimes, you have to do it for you. Aligning your heart and mind means retraining your brain to support your inner self. Fight *for* your feelings rather than against them, and don't worry what anyone else thinks. You're the only one who has to live your life. Don't let your busy, bossy brain order you around like an extra. You are the star in your own movie.

Humans are actually the only species on the planet that over-analyze their feelings. Animals will go off their instincts without question and act immediately. They won't waste time obsessing about why they got a certain feeling and whether they should do something about it. We're all taught to think logically and to deny our impulses. But what if we listened to them? Our decisions should be more based off of our instincts. It's our inner core trying to communicate with us – with no filter, nothing clouding it.

When all the different aspects of yourself – mental, emotional and physical – are in alignment, there's no limit to what you can achieve.

Try to live a truly spontaneous day. Treat this as a game. Experiment with it and see what happens.

Whatever comes up during the day – whatever requests are made or opportunities are on offer – Just. Say. Yes.

You might be familiar with the idea from the Jim Carrey movie *Yes Man*. It might be classed as a comedy, but there's a heck of a message there in the story! The idea of making "Yes" into a rule is to give yourself permission to let go of the usual negativity we can be prey to and experiment with the complexity of the decision-making process. There can be lots of variations made to the ongoing rule, but for one day, just try the simplest version.

Go with it and see what happens!

Interestingly, it was proved in my wife's business not long ago how effective having this "yes" mentality can really be. Krissy received an email with a business opportunity. She thought it through, letting her brain come up with all the reasons not to go for it, and decided to dismiss it. She deleted the email, but the next day, something told her to tell me about it anyway. I immediately pounced on the opportunity. My gut gave me the thumbs up and my "yes" brain, aligned with my heart, backed it up. Instead of fighting the feeling and entering into the reasons she shouldn't, I asked, why shouldn't she? So much could come from it! Krissy took the email out the trash and embarked on a business relationship that has been unbelievably rewarding. Through saying "yes" where she'd normally say "no," amazing things have happened.

Now, the thing is, Krissy was indirectly listening to her intuition! Her brain did its usual job and came up with all the logical excuses, leading to her original, rational course of action. However, that nagging little voice inside wouldn't let go. Knowing me as well as she does, she must have subconsciously known I would be full steam ahead for the idea! And when that little voice told her to talk to me about it, even though she'd already put the email in the trash, she listened, because deep down inside, she wanted to go for it. So she let her inner self speak, and together we went with the course of action that *really* felt right – the one that aligned heart and mind!

So whatever comes up for you during this experiment, don't think through the logical rationale. Don't find all the excuses not to do something – just do it. You'll soon want to live like this every day! See what comes up for you and record it in your journal.

4 DESIGN YOUR ENVIRONMENT

The concept of controlling your surroundings is really a microcosm of the entire message of this book – that you can create your reality. It is a great element to play with, because your surroundings are a physical representation of your life where you can experience any change you make in a really concrete way – seeing, hearing, touching, smelling, even tasting the difference in your external world with immediate effect.

There are three elements to your environment in this context: places, people and media. The first is the most obvious, but the latter two are perhaps more important. The biggest hijackers of your mind, time and motivation are actually the people that you hang out with and the media. Your mind is your compass. The people you hang out with and the media can direct it if you allow them to.

Again, the point I'm going to hammer home is that your circumstances are your choice. Regardless of where you live and work now, regardless of whom you surround yourself with, regardless of how you spend your time on social media – you are in control. You can choose your biggest influences – you dictate where you spend your time and whom you spend it with. You can relocate yourself away from toxic environments and toxic people, and you needn't waste one moment feeling bad about it. This is real back-to-basics stuff, but it needs to be said. When it comes to enabling your success and achieving your vision – you can choose to make it easier to get there.

CHOOSE YOUR PLACES

This aspect of your environment is really open to interpretation. It might be your house or the kind of places you hang out. It might be your whole town or country! You might not want to change anything major, but I bet there are one or two aspects of your immediate surroundings, even if they're minor, that you could tweak for the better. What's important to understand is that the places where you spend your time are within your control.

You might hate your house and wish you could move – and perhaps it's not possible to do that overnight, so make it part of your vision! Maybe it's the climate you don't like or the locality. What do you love doing? If it's surfing, for example, why only do it on vacation? Why not move to the beach and surf every day, or as much as you want, even if it's before or after a day's work? The same if you love to ski and the ski vacation is the highlight of your year. Why not move to the mountains?

Some of you will be happy where you are and might look at your more immediate surroundings. There are those who swear by the effects of clearing away clutter in the home for increasing their levels of happiness and productivity. Some go so far as to become proponents of feng shui.

Others just need to get outside more. The benefits of biophilia – connecting with nature – have been proved beyond all doubt. Whether it's taking more walks in the park, cultivating a garden or just bringing some greenery into your home, try it and see what kind of difference it makes.

exercise: Change Places

Take stock of your surroundings and decide whether there's anything you want to change. If you're thinking, *Well, obviously, I'd rather live in a mansion on a beach in a hot country somewhere* (and if you're serious about it!), then make it a part of your vision. Write about it in your journal. Go on vacation and smell the leather, so to speak. (I relate smelling the leather to when I drove a Ferrari for the first time: I know how it smells, how it drives, how it sounds, how it shifts and, above all, the exhilarating feeling I had when I drove it!) So, experience this luxurious beach life and all its charms. The warmer climate, the sea right next door, the myriad things you can enjoy, from a walk on the beach at sunset to catching a wave to the freshest, finest seafood at dinner. Put up pictures, make it your screensaver, talk about the home you'd like to make there. Experience the details of your beach-life routine as if you're already there, enjoying *your* beach house, *as if when without*, and make the vision part of what you're moving towards. Make a mind movie!

Perhaps, in the meantime, do a de-cluttering experiment! Get rid of things you haven't used or worn in so long that it's pointless having them around – whether that's against the wall in the hallway, on top of a table or at the back of a cupboard. Clean out your life and make it a cathartic experience. Surround yourself only with things you love and make your home a place you truly enjoy being in.

At the same time, if you don't get outside much, plan to do so. Take a trip to the park or make a hike a part of your weekly routine. Breathe some fresh air. Get out there and see what swimming in a freshwater lake is like or experience sunset somewhere you can see the horizon. Wherever you are, there'll be greenery *somewhere*, even if you have to commute to it. Make the effort and see how you feel for it. You never know whom you might bump into, as well.

Now, as part of your daily routine, regardless of what other changes you make, I want to add a drill. This is a drill to practice every morning. It helps you build situational awareness and become alert to your surroundings. It's an army drill I learned from Retired Lt. Col Scott Mann, an ex Green Beret who spent eighteen years in Special Forces and twenty-three in the U.S. Army.

1. Stop:

- Each morning, find a quiet spot outside.
- Crouch down and take the soil or rocks into your fingers.
- Allow yourself to slip into the role of predator.

2. Look:

- Scan your horizon from left to right, then right to left, slowly. Take it all in the way a big cat surveys the landscape from a tree branch.

3. Listen:

- Close your eyes.

- Listen for the most distant sound.
- Picture it in your mind as if you are floating above it.
- Listen for the closest sound.

4. Smell:

- Take in every smell that you can.
- What belongs?
- What doesn't?

CHOOSE YOUR PEOPLE

It is said that you are the average of the five people closest to you, the ones you hang out with on a regular basis. If the people you spend most time with are your pals at work, and they live for their pay check, going straight to the shops on a Friday and then to a bar for apps and drinks, chances are you're with them.

If all your friends live a healthy lifestyle, work out, eat right and have amazing bodies, chances are you do the same and have a great body too! Birds of a feather flock together.

It's important to be around like-minded people. So if you're trying to reprogram your mind, you need to be around people with your desired mindset. You can try to do it all yourself, but my question to you is: Why? It's a lot easier to accomplish something with the help and support of another person, even more so with a team.

If you surround yourself with people hungry for the same things you want, who have met success doing the things you want to do, then you're more likely to achieve your vision. You want to be around people who are positive, motivated, healthy, genuine, authentic, enthusiastic and, most important, supportive, because they understand what you're trying to achieve. This is how you level up!

It may sound harsh, but you need to cut the dead wood in your life. People who don't support your intentions are success-sucking vampires. When you're trying to boost your self-belief, it's no good hanging around people who are going to put down you and your desires for their own insecure reasons. People who are closed off from the idea of there being possibilities beyond the daily dredge are the ones who love to close doors in people's faces. Instead, you want to seek the company of those people who love to open doors for others. They are the ones who will enable your dreams.

It is so incredibly hard to make a change – any change – if the people around you are doing something completely different. Your environment doesn't support it. You need to design an environment that does.

exercise: Guard Your Time

Do you have any people around you who are perpetually negative? They're always down on everything. Their perspective is that things always suck. They never have a good time, even when good things are going on. They don't recognize the positives in their lives, but always lament the world being against them. They *always* get the raw deal. Bad stuff *always* happens to them.

More than that, when people try to help them, they argue their right to fail. I can think of one old acquaintance in particular here. They came to me for advice on how to get healthier and fitter, because they had been unwell and their doctor had advised that improving their nutrition and implementing an exercise regimen would help. I gave my guidance freely, taking the time to go through a program with them that I would usually charge for in the normal course of business. Because it seemed like too much hard work, they devalued what they'd been given, arguing all the reasons these changes wouldn't work for them instead of trying to implement them. They did their own thing, which wasn't very much at all, and saw no improvement in their health and fitness. When they were next unwell, they didn't see it as their responsibility – it was life delivering them hard knocks again.

These are the kind of people who, if you told them about this book, they'd pooh pooh you. They'd call you out as crazy for having a vision, scoff at you, make you feel foolish and small. If you're fired up about something, they're the ones who douse the flames.

Don't give these people your time. If they're always asking for favors, try the opposite of the exercise in the last chapter, and say "no." If they want to spend time with you or start chewing your ear off about something, be busy. Have another commitment. Go and do something else. Stop giving them your time and they will eventually stop asking for it. They'll stop taking it. Your energy levels will go up and so will your goodwill. Spend your time with people who will boost you up, not drag you down.

Of course, it's not always as simple as cutting people out of your life. Some of your biggest critics may be family members! And you probably *have* to spend time with them. But you choose how much energy you give them. You choose how they affect you. You choose whether they stop you from doing something, and how much time you spend thinking about their overt or implied criticism when you're not around them. Love your family and choose your friends. You can succeed in spite of them.

CHOOSE YOUR MEDIA

These days, we're facing something truly unprecedented – a disconnection paradox. Digitally, we are more connected than ever, but we're spending more time face-to-face with our screens, our heads in "the cloud," engaging with people and news online, than we are actually conversing with people face-to-face, doing things together, or being out in nature. Even when we are out with other people, we're instantly cataloging it and advertising the fact to the Internet, tagging the time, the place, the participants. We live in FOMO ("fear of missing out"), constantly checking our "feed" and seeing what everyone else is up to. We're always up to date with the latest developments, and have commented on the most popular memes, but we're disengaged and disconnected from what's really important. It's not just that we're distracted – that implies our usual state is something else. We're in a constant state of distraction. Even addiction.

Just watch Dr. Cal Newport's TEDx talk on quitting social media, and you'll see that not only does it not spell the end of the world, but it could actually do the opposite – it could save you. Dr. Newport describes himself as a rarity – a millennial, computer scientist and book author standing on a TED stage who has never had a social media account. He goes through the common objections he gets faced with when he suggests quitting, and, in his words, "defuses the hype."

Firstly, social media is not a fundamental technology – it is a source of entertainment. Rejecting this form of entertainment in favor of others is not about taking a social stance that projects you back into the dark ages. It is about – you guessed it – simply making a choice. Dr. Newport relays the fact that many of the major social media companies hire "attention engineers" who borrow techniques used by Vegas casinos to try to make their offering as addictive as possible. This maximizes the profit that can be extracted from your attention and data. In terms of the entertainment it embodies, Dr. Newport wants you to recognize that social media is on the more unsavory side. Even Steve Jobs recognized the addictive nature of tech. Though he invented the iPad, he wouldn't let his children use it! And he's not the only powerful person in the tech world to have limited their kids' use of technology.

Secondly, not building your own social media brand doesn't necessarily disadvantage you in today's economy; it doesn't mean you won't be found or followed or presented with opportunities. Dr. Newport authored a book called *Deep Work*, which makes the point that what the market values is the ability to produce things that are rare and valuable. Meanwhile, the market dismisses activities that are easy to replicate and don't produce much value. Social media, he points out, is the epitome of an activity that is easy to replicate and doesn't produce much value. He argues that this behavior isn't going to be rewarded. Instead, the market is going to reward "the deep, concentrated work required to build real skills and to apply those skills to produce things like a craftsman that are rare and that are valuable." If you can do that deep work, put in that kind of deep effort, you will be found, you will be presented with opportunities, and you will be rewarded.

Finally, social media brings with it "multiple, well-documented, significant harms." It is designed to fragment your attention, and this can permanently reduce your capacity for concentration. It isn't just harmless fun. Psychologically, it is documented that constant use can lead to feelings of isolation, that exposing yourself endlessly to the filtered, curated versions of your friends' lives can lead to feelings of inadequacy and increase rates of depression. Levels of anxiety have risen on college campuses since the ubiquitous use of smartphones – and Dr. Newport calls this the canary in the coalmine. There are signs all around us that social media can be dangerous.

Meanwhile, on the other side of the coin, the doctor argues that when we respect our attention, the benefits are monumental. We are able to truly concentrate and, thence, trade intensity for time. He says his life outside of work is ... peaceful. Restorative. There isn't all this constant stimulus and the hum of anxiety that goes along with it.

I can honestly say that when I shut off the amount of time I spent with media in general, my life changed for the better. The first few days were a little tough because it was habit to keep checking CNN (constant negative news!). But now, because of the person I have become, I will never go back. I truly don't have time. My time is spent accomplishing my vision.

Shut off some of the noise that surrounds you and you'll find yourself not only with more time, but more awareness when it comes to what's really important.

A lot of things in life happen through conversations with the right kind of people. In a world that is now constantly tweeting, posing and posting on Facebook, interpersonal communication has taken a back seat. If you want to get more out of life, put yourself in the right environment. Start having one-on-one conversations in person and build real rapport – you will be amazed at the results.

Most people want to be interesting; they want to fit in. Try being *interested* in others instead of being interesting, and stop trying to control your conversations. Be someone whom others want to be around. Make others feel special.

The media has a great business model – it hooks you so advertisers will keep paying huge sums of money to the various platforms. Want to change your life right now? Stop watching the news, stop accessing your social media, stop engaging through likes and shares, and start taking action. Take that time and energy and apply it to changing your reality!

Think you can't go cold turkey? Try to phase it out. When you're working on a task, stop yourself from taking these "micro-breaks" where you go and browse.

It's the same as when you're a kid studying. You get bored, so you keep breaking to go and check the fridge. Nothing will have changed in there since the last time you looked! Social media's the same.

If you don't already have a "no devices at the dinner table" rule, then introduce one! No device in the bedroom is a good one too. Don't let the last thing you do when you go to bed and the first thing you do when you wake up be a scroll through social media.

If you really recognize the addiction's got you, try using a couple of the tools that have become available to help, such as SelfControl. This is a Mac application that helps you avoid distracting websites. You give it a list of sites and put a timer on it and it will block your bad habits. For more inspiration, check out this article at eCampus: http://www.ecampusnews.com/featured/featured-on-ecampus-news/apps-mobile-distractions/. It lists ten apps to help you block device distractions.

5 LOOK AFTER YOURSELF

I could write a whole book on the subject of this step, and, in fact, I've already begun such a project! Health and wellness is the third of my foundational pillars. In terms of living a life of quantum success, it couldn't be more important.

Again, we're really going back to basics. There are three integral elements to building a better you, and they are: nutrition, exercise and recovery. Success really isn't possible without having these aspects in balance. The mind is truly connected to the body. The better you look after your body, the more your mind can thrive! As it's the mind that has the power to alter your reality, and the body that's the tool to take the appropriate action, taking care of both of them is a no-brainer.

Whatever you do, don't tell yourself you don't have time to put simple changes into effect. What you're really saying is you don't want to! There's no such thing as not having time – only not prioritizing your time.

If someone says they don't have time to go to the right place to buy healthy food, don't have time to exercise, and couldn't possibly get more rest, it's time to catalog a week in their life – hour by hour – and see what activities are taking up all the time there is in each day. I can guarantee that there will be opportunity to replace some unhealthy activities with healthy ones. The time is available – it just has to be reapportioned.

Your beliefs around time are what make the difference. Don't dwell in the past or future. All you have is now. In fact, you have an abundance of now – so do something with it. This is actually one of the easiest of all the steps to take – you can physically put it into practice right away and feeling the benefits doesn't come far behind. Why wouldn't you?

NUTRITION

Let's start with basic nutrition. It's very simple, to be honest. The body only cares about caloric balance. The more calories you consume, the more calories you have to burn. If not, you gain weight. If you burn more calories than you ingest, you lose weight.

Nutrition is the staple and key ingredient in any high-performance lifestyle program. There is no "magic pill" when it comes to your diet, which was a disappointment for the huge number of clients in the past who would always ask for one! However, there are some straightforward recommendations that you can put into practice with ease.

I always use the KISS method – keep it simple, stupid! Here are ten pieces of advice right off the bat:

DO:

1. Drink plenty of water.
2. Buy natural and organic produce wherever possible.
3. Eat fruits and vegetables, especially leafy greens.
4. Eat yogurt for probiotics and drink green tea for antioxidants.
5. Choose lean cuts of meat and eat fish a couple of times a week.

DON'T:

1. Purchase processed and prepared food, especially fast food.
2. Eat foods high in sodium and sugar.
3. Eat foods high in cholesterol and low in fiber.
4. Drink soda, juice or any other beverages that are high in sugar or fructose corn syrup.
5. Drink much alcohol, if at all.

EXERCISE

Being a Strength and Conditioning Specialist, there are so many exercises I want to share that can help you through the phases to becoming a high-performance person – that's part of the reason a whole book on the subject is in the pipeline! For the purposes of this step, however, I'm going to keep it simple for you.

Your fitness can't be neglected. You have to *move*. Moving gets your mind going as well as your body. You have to move every day in some way, shape or form, and it's best if you have a routine to follow. It's about forming positive habits – making small changes at first, but seeing the snowball effect when you stick with them and keep making improvements.

Perhaps you're already super active ... but don't be alarmed if, at the moment, you don't move much at all. It's easy to build it up.

The days where people would commit to body-building workouts, aerobics and slow cardio for hours at a time at the gym are largely over – no one sees themselves as having time.

The demand is for workouts that can be completed within thirty to fifty minutes, with the option of exercising at home. They have to be functional, effective and keep you healthy, while also helping to prevent injuries. You don't want to just be moving on one plane of motion – repeating the same activity over and over. Life is multi-planer, so your routines should be the same!

There is so much to choose from right now in the fitness world. It's a lot like nutritional guidance – new fads are everywhere! It makes you wonder who's right. A word of caution: Just because something looks crazy, makes people stare, or makes you feel like you've worked so hard you want to throw up – it doesn't necessarily mean it's good for you. Sometimes, it's the opposite.

The best thing to do is grab the bull by the horns and take action. See what sorts of activities suit you. You can research, read and question everything in the world about working out and gaining fitness, but, at the end of the day, absorbing vast amounts of theory isn't going to help you. It all comes down to you taking that first step and taking action.

To start you off, here's one thing you could put into action right away: Get yourself a thirty-six to forty-one-inch trampoline. This will enable you to put a full body exercise into practice every day, with minimum effort.

The reason I've suggested buying something is that this very act of investing in your health will motivate you to take action! It will be there looking at you every day. Rebounding is a significant part of my daily mobility routine, and it's the perfect start because it's fun.

The best part is that this size of trampoline is easy to pack and travel with, so you can perform this exercise anywhere – your bedroom, basement, office, yard, even on vacation – even if it's only for a couple minutes every couple of hours.

It's best to start with a few minutes and work your way up to ten or more minutes each morning. Ideally, you should try to do four ten-minute sessions or two twenty-minute sessions a day – this will get you optimal results.

Still not convinced? Here are ten benefits of rebounding, aside from its convenience:

1. It is more than twice as effective as running, without the extra stress on the ankles and knees.

2. It increases agility.
3. It improves digestion.
4. It boosts lymphatic drainage and the immune function.
5. It increases endurance on a cellular level by stimulating mitochondrial production (these are responsible for cell energy).
6. It improves balance by stimulating the vestibule in the middle ear.
7. It improves muscle strength and tone.
8. It supports the skeletal system and increases bone mass.
9. It helps support the thyroid and adrenals.
10. It helps circulate oxygen throughout the body, increasing energy levels, rejuvenating the body when tired.

For more exercises and best-practice training videos, access the resources at QuantumPersonalSafety.com.

RECOVERY

The importance of rest cannot be exaggerated. When you're asleep, that's when your body's parasympathetic system (part of your nervous system) repairs the different parts of your body and replenishes your cells. The effects of sleep deprivation are well documented; there's a reason it's been used as a form of torture! The more rested your body and mind, the better they perform.

I wake up every morning without an alarm. Seems crazy, right? I'm sure you're shaking your head, but it *is* possible. I know a lot of people who can do it. And so can you. It's actually a sign that you're getting enough sleep!

Most people rely on an alarm because they don't go to bed at a reasonable hour, so the key is to make sure you are going to bed when you feel tired. Your body knows when it's time; unfortunately, most people just don't listen. If you want to get up at a decent hour, a good time to go to bed is always before 10pm. The night before, prepare to wake up the next morning by visualizing the experience and focusing on the exact time you want to awaken.

If you do insist on using an alarm, I would recommend one that is gentle, such as a vibration, chime or a light that slowly becomes brighter. The reason you shouldn't use a loud alarm is because the sudden jolt into wakefulness is not natural; the waking process should be gentle.

Here are ten tips for getting yourself a proper night's sleep:

DO:

1. Sleep in a quiet, cool, dark room.
2. Have a regular schedule – go to bed at the same time every day.
3. Do some form of exercise every day.

4. Replace your mattress if it is old and worn out.
5. Use your bed only for reading, sleeping and sex.

DON'T:

1. Take late-afternoon naps.
2. Drink much alcohol, if at all. Don't drink during the two hours before bed.
3. Eat a huge meal and try to fall asleep on a full stomach.
4. Have stimulants, such as caffeine and tobacco, after 2-3pm, if at all.
5. Sit yourself in front of a screen right before bed – don't work on your laptop, watch TV or read from a smart device.

exercise: Adopt Healthy Habits

I want you to open a new document or start a new notebook. This is going to be your health and wellness journal, keeping a record of your daily diet, exercise and sleep patterns. Don't combine this with your Quantum Success Journal; it is easier to draw comparisons if, page on page, you just have a simple summary and you can flick back and forth to pages with the same format.

When you first start this, your more unhealthy habits are going to jump right out at you. The key is going to be making small changes every day until this journal reflects the eating, exercising and sleeping habits of a high-performance person!

Each day, for thirty days, list the following:

- **Nutrition:** Make a note of everything you eat, including the portion sizes, the time of day and even the reason. (Were you seriously hungry, were you bored or feeling low, or were you eating because everyone else was?)

- **Exercise:** Make a note of each activity you do and for how long.

- **Recovery:** Make a note of when you go to bed, when you wake and how you feel your quality of sleep was.

- **Energy:** Write down how you felt the day before. This way, you can correlate having energy with the foods you are eating and the amount of sleep you had the night before. You'll see if some foods are affecting you in a negative way.

Day by day, circle your bad habits. Start putting the tips from the three sections into practice, and soon you'll see fewer and fewer circles. Make yourself a routine to stick to and see the change in your performance day by day!

6 BREAK DOWN YOUR BARRIERS

Most people are experts at using their mind to imagine negative outcomes. They could see some amazing results in their lives if they used their mind to pursue positive thoughts the same way they do negative ones. They don't realize that it's possible to reprogram your mind and replace the negative default program. It takes the same amount of energy to produce negative or positive thoughts. It's just as easy to be successful as it is to be unsuccessful!

For most people, all that's limiting them is their beliefs. Whether you think you can or you think you can't – it actually doesn't matter. Both beliefs are correct. If you think you can't do something, you won't. If you think you can do something, you will.

Now, in order to be able to change them, it's important to first understand what beliefs are and how they are created.

A belief is your attitude toward something. It is a statement of "truth" you have created for yourself, usually through taking on the belief of someone else. It's a thought to which you have attached a deep-rooted feeling.

For example, a belief could be that talking to strangers is bad. You might believe this because of years of repetition – your parents, teachers and relatives will have beaten it into your mind that talking to strangers is bad and your mind has taken up the chant. It's become an attitude associated with strong emotions.

In reality, if I don't know you, should I automatically assume you are bad? Think about it; despite what we've all been taught, a stranger isn't automatically a danger. A stranger can help save your life. Meanwhile, as the statistics on violence show, it's the people we haven't categorized as "danger" who often pose the biggest threat.

It's important to understand this because other people and things don't really create your beliefs. You are the only person who can create a belief. And if you have the power to create it, you have the power to control it.

DEFEAT LIMITING BELIEFS

Lots of information gets presented to us through our senses; it all goes into our brain where it is processed and a belief is created. Your brain truly doesn't know the difference between a real and imagined experience. All your brain has to refer to when it comes to making decisions about anything is the information that it receives. It's what you do inside your brain that really matters.

Let's use my wife as a real-life example – I do this in my personal safety book as well because it's such a good illustration. My wife has had a fear of public speaking since college, because she once had a bad experience. She would still talk about how much she hated speaking in front of large groups of people many years later.

That was due to her experience. The information in her mind was that she gave a talk in front of some other students and it didn't go well. What came next were the feelings and emotions that your brain releases when you experience an event. Let's say you process the information and tell yourself that it was bad, scary and nerve-wracking, as most people would.

When you've processed the event you've experienced, you start to feel the associated emotions run through you. The result is that the mind associates speaking in front of groups of people with the negative emotions running through you, such as embarrassment, shame and fear.

However, in reality, an event is just an event. It's your beliefs about the event that peg it as bad or good. You could have 1,000 people witness an event and possibly have 1,000 different beliefs about the outcome of that event.

The experience itself doesn't really matter; that is just the information going to your brain. What matters is what happens with the information once it gets to your brain.

The first thing my wife did was categorize standing up in front of a classroom and speaking as scary and bad, which allowed her body to feel those negative emotions. What she did was create the root of a belief in her brain.

So, for her, the root of the belief is that public speaking results in her feeling extreme nervousness, embarrassment and fear. Every time she thinks about public speaking or tells anyone her feelings about it, she replays that negative experience over and over in her mind, and reinforces the belief.

Sometimes, it only takes one negative experience to form a limiting belief.

Take a moment and reflect on this point. Can you think of any of your own limiting beliefs? Can you trace them back to their roots?

This is the illustration I use when it comes to personal safety: Imagine two women who have equal physical skills but differing belief systems about their abilities. The woman who believes she will prevail against her attacker will. The woman who doesn't believe in herself has the odds greatly stacked against her.

The most important piece of advice here is that everything must be aligned. Your belief system needs to correlate to your mental and physical abilities. The mind navigates the body. When it comes to personal safety, if you don't believe you can prevail against your attacker, you won't – no matter how much knowledge you attain or skills you possess. It's exactly the same when it comes to your personal development. Having limiting beliefs and self-doubt will block you when it's time for you to take action in order to achieve your vision, so you need to work through such beliefs.

Let's look at some examples of limiting beliefs:

- No one else around me is looking for more; I should be content with what I've got, even if I yearn for something different. My peers will judge me and think I'm getting above myself if I try.
- The people I consider successful all have something I don't; there's no way I can be like them. I don't have what it takes; if I try and I fail, it will be shameful.
- It's not possible to get what you want all the time; that's a fairytale. If I go for it, I'll be kidding myself and I'll end up looking foolish.
- I'm not educated enough to attain the level of wealth and influence I imagine having.
- I'm too old to change anything now; dreams are for children.

These are limiting beliefs that will hold you back from doing whatever you can to succeed. Take, for example, the belief that because no one else from your neighborhood has ever started their own business successfully, you won't be able to or, worse, don't deserve to. Holding such a belief can cause you to give up the fight before it's even begun. It is defeatist. It doesn't take into account that everyone is individual and there are principles that you can put into play to succeed, one of which is envisioning a different outcome for yourself.

Just by challenging such beliefs you can begin to turn the tables and align yourself with what you *can* do, rather than becoming their prisoner.

This is the really important part about understanding your mind and changing your mindset. Each and every time you replay something in your mind, your brain takes it for a "real" experience. Whether it is happening in the physical world or only in your head, it is no different. This is how the information is processed.

It's like walking the same way through the snow over and over again – eventually you will make a path that becomes the quickest and easiest route to follow.

Most people don't understand how their mind works and let themselves fall into this trap as a result. However, once you understand the way your mind works, it means you can trick your brain. You can completely reverse limiting beliefs by manipulating how your brain works.

To put it simply, if you can imagine something inside your mind, your mind will assume it is real. By controlling how your emotions respond to the thought, you will start developing a belief about something, even if this runs counter to a belief you already hold. Through a process of repetition, you can replace the old belief with a new one.

My wife reprogrammed her mind when it came to public speaking. She went over and over the association of being relaxed, confident and even ecstatic about public speaking, to the point where the idea of speaking in front of people elicited a positive emotional response. She strengthened the association between public speaking and positive emotions instead of negative ones. By applying these tools, she has been able to reverse her limiting belief.

By revisiting specific limiting beliefs and putting them into different scenarios where this belief is upended, we can entirely reprogram our mind with new beliefs.

We can turn these new beliefs into positive affirmations.

PRACTICE POSITIVE AFFIRMATIONS

Forming positive affirmations is sometimes called constructive imagination. When you construct your affirmations, you want to identify exactly what it is that you want to develop and strengthen, then attach positive emotions to it.

So how do you write and use them? First, make sure your affirmations are specific and in the present tense. The most important point when constructing them is to make sure you write them as if you are already achieving the result. I suggest starting out with just a few, then adding more over time, and not making them too long – no longer than a couple of lines.

Your affirmations should be practiced upon waking and right before you fall asleep at night, because that is when your mind is quiet and relaxed. I make this part of my daily high-performance routine.

Crucially, make sure you don't just read them. You have to feel deep inside that you have already achieved the affirmation.

Let's revisit our examples of limiting beliefs and turn them into positive affirmations:

- I look at life differently from the people around me and it means I have everything I ever yearn for.
- There's no difference between the people I consider successful and me; I'm a success story just like them.
- There's no such thing as an impossible dream. Success is not a fairy tale; it's my core value.
- I guide my own education and learn exactly what I need when I need to.
- Dreams are for everyone; it's exactly the right time for me to be changing my life.

Open your Quantum Success Journal and write down the limiting beliefs that are holding you back. Trace these to their root and understand what influences have made you think that way. Now, draw a line through each of them. Cross them out – even rip out the page or delete them completely if you're using a word processor – and don't think about them again.

On a fresh page, write down your own set of affirmations. Go through them as many times as you need to throughout your day, making sure not to skip the two most important times of day – before falling asleep and upon waking.

7 REFRAME FAILURE

I love seeing my kids fail.

That might seem counter-intuitive. Aren't my kids upset when they fail? Well, sure they are – at first. But we're bringing them up to understand that there's a bigger picture at play here. Without things going wrong sometimes, without *doing* things wrong sometimes, there's no personal growth. It's through overcoming challenges and obstacles that we learn. Learning from our mistakes, as well as other people's mistakes, is one of the most important things we can do in order to progress.

What is failure, really? You *could* call it the opposite of success. It's falling short of something, or the act of something breaking. It refers to something that has not gone as planned and achieved the desired outcome. *I failed* is a phrase full of negative connotations marking someone's inability to complete a task.

However, this definition overlooks the vast importance of trial and error when it comes to discovering a successful solution. There must be an infinite number of examples, but Edison is my favorite. Allegedly, his teachers at school labeled him too stupid to learn anything, and it took him a thousand iterations to create a working light bulb. However, when a reporter asked him how it felt to fail a thousand times, his reply encompassed what "failure" can really mean. He said he hadn't really failed a thousand times – the light bulb was an invention with a thousand steps.

Don't give up! Persist! Have people shaking their heads over your obstinacy. *That's* how you get somewhere. If you fail, shake it off. It isn't the end of the road; it's just a step along it. The universe rewards those who keep going, who keep asking, who keep trying – even when they've failed. There is no greater education than failure.

PERMISSION TO FAIL

How do you reframe failure? It's about a shift in perspective. Saying it's okay to fail is like saying it's okay to quit ... and it is – if you're quitting something that's bad for you! Believing it's okay to fail is fine – if you believe that failure's good for you.

Creating your own reality is about turning these norms on their head. It's about changing the way you look at things to your own advantage. Naturally, the more you try to do something, the more you're going to fail at it. And that's a good thing! It means you're committed, like Edison, to getting it right in the end. The more you try, the more you will fail, but, also, the more likely you will be to succeed.

Once you've got it right, all that came before is completely reframed by your success. Achieving what you want in the end means that you were never really a failure! Just look at Steve Jobs, considered one of the most successful people to have passed through this world. In his 2005 Stanford commencement speech, he told three stories. The first was about connecting the dots. He described how dropping out of college meant attending classes he would never otherwise have been able to attend, and how, ten years later, what seemed like a class with no future application, calligraphy, shaped the game-changing Macintosh. He said, "Much of what I stumbled into by following my curiosity and intuition turned out to be priceless later on... You have to trust that the dots will somehow connect in your future."

His second story was about love and loss. Steve Jobs was fired from Apple, the company *he* founded, at the age of thirty. He called himself "a very public failure." He could have "run away from the valley" and he could have given it all up, but he realized that he loved what he did. Embracing his new creative freedom, he went on to found Pixar and NeXT, which, strangely enough, Apple went on to acquire, bringing him back into the fold. In that time, he also met his wife, and he attributed it all to this devastating failure – being fired from Apple. He even called it the best thing that could have ever happened to him. He said, "Sometimes, life's going to hit you in the head with a brick. Don't lose faith."

What could be a better example of overcoming failure and reframing it? At thirty, Steve Jobs was the biggest failure he knew! He felt like he had let down the next generation of entrepreneurs. He had been turfed out of the company that he himself had built and made so successful. But so many incredible things that went on to happen wouldn't have been possible without this bump in the road. Failure was success in disguise, and it was only later, joining the dots looking back, that this made sense.

The final story in his Stanford address was about death. This is something else you can reframe – you don't have to look at death as being the end of your journey. Instead, you can look at it as being what gives life its meaning. It is inevitable and, if you look at it in a certain way, motivational. Steve Jobs said, "Almost everything, all external expectations, all pride, all fear of embarrassment or failure, these things just fall away in the face of death, leaving only what is truly important. Remembering that you are going to die is the best way I know to avoid the trap of thinking you have something to lose."

You are going to die one day, and you are going to fail a whole bunch before that day. But that's great! How amazing is it that we have this life and this chance to shine? How amazing is it that we have this opportunity to learn, to reframe failure and step past it on our way to success?

TURN FAILURE INTO SUCCESS

One afternoon, I picked up my son Peter and two of his friends and took them up the mountain to go skiing. Now, to get into the main parking lot where I was dropping the boys off, you have to go up a steep, one-way road to the entrance. The exit is at the other end of the parking lot. As I was driving up, a car came down the hill the wrong way, driving dangerously straight towards me. I could have swerved out of the way, but I got hooked by anger. I held my ground, playing a game of chicken. The other driver pulled over to the side of the road. Reaching the front of the lot to drop the boys off, I saw in my rear-view mirror that the driver of the vehicle had turned his car around and was racing back up the road towards me.

My heart started to race. I told the boys to stay in the truck and got out. The driver rolled down his window and began yelling at me for almost hitting him. I yelled back that he was the one going the wrong way down a one-way street and that he put our lives in danger because he was too lazy to read the signs or go out the right exit. I told him to get the heck out of there and he left.

When I calmed down, I felt absolutely horrible. I'd completely failed to control my emotions. Even though I had perceived myself to be in the right, I quickly realized I could have handled things a completely different way.

Failure is going to happen to you once in a while – you are going to fail. Like I said, life isn't a straight line. But it's what you do with it that matters. It's whether you use it as an excuse to quit, and keep failing, or learn from it. When you learn from your mistakes, you realize that failure is education.

I want to share the rest of my entry in my Quantum Success Journal to show you how to really look at yourself and your actions. It's possible to learn from the things that go wrong – even the things that *you* do wrong – and find yourself in a better position because of that act of self-reflection. With the experience behind you, you can then choose how to act going forward.

I learned a great deal from this encounter:

1. *I am human and made a mistake. Granted, the boys were in the truck and the driver had put them in danger but I should never have responded in the fashion. As a personal safety instructor as well as someone who has had extensive coaching in getting unhooked from emotions, I shouldn't have allowed my emotions to take over.*
2. *I wasn't feeling 100% and I took it out on a stranger who could have made an honest mistake and really not seen the Do Not Enter signs.*
3. *I can use this mistake as a teaching tool for myself and my son. No one is perfect. I am human and make mistakes – everybody does. It's what you do with it that matters.*
4. *You can meditate, train, be awakened, and learn about personal growth all you want, but applying it in the moment is the true test.*

5. *Next time, I will unhook from the emotion and act appropriately, keeping a level head.*

The trick is to look at events that unfold for learning and growing opportunities, but then let go of the past. The past doesn't exist! If you come from a place of fear – fear of failure, fear of not being enough – and you are always looking back at events that entrench you in this fear, then all you get is more fear. The world becomes a fearful place to be. However, if you come from a place of unconditional love and live in each moment, letting life meet you half way, then you put yourself in a position to succeed.

When I talk about unconditional love, I'm talking about love with no rules. There's no condition saying, "If this, then that." It's the difference between admiring the flowers in a valley for their inherent beauty versus the commercial value you could get from picking them and turning them into perfume. You can love everything as it is – not for how it serves your needs.

Don't crumble when something goes wrong. Get creative instead. When life throws you challenges, it's only going to make you stronger. It leads you down the path you are supposed to be going down. There is a magical reason why and you just have to see it. Like Steve Jobs said, you can't connect the dots looking forward – you can only connect them looking backwards. That's when the meaning of everything you've gone through becomes clear. Everything was needed to get you to this point and make you who you are.

Too many people look at challenges and problems as negative when, in reality, challenges are HUGE positives. They really are – you just have to look at them with a different set of glasses. When you look at life as a game, you realize you're going to lose a hand sometimes – but that doesn't mean you give up and stop playing. Have fun with it and keep going and you can accomplish amazing things!

exercise: Reframe Failure

This is one of life's biggest challenges, because the fear of failure is one of the main culprits for holding people back. People hate to look foolish, and being knocked back is a horrible prospect. It's all very well and good to say you ought to accept that failure will be a part of your reality and that you need to reframe it as an opportunity to learn, but how do you do that in practice? This is the way you overcome failure and become all the stronger for it.

This is where your Quantum Success Journal is truly priceless. You don't want to dwell on failure or the prospect of failure – that only attracts more failure. But you do need to work through it in order to reap the benefits. These benefits might not appear right away; you may only be able to connect the dots looking back. However, you need to write about your failure as though you have already learned the lesson to come and gotten the value from it.

In your journal, start by describing a failure from your past, where you can already connect the dots and see how it led you down a path you might not have otherwise travelled. What lesson did you learn? What great thing happened that wouldn't have happened otherwise?

Next, day by day, catalog your failures in a similar way, whether major or minor. State your intent to learn from them, grow from them, and look back and be able to teach from them. Do not dwell on what went wrong; focus on the perspective that you have already overcome it and that it has done you good – rewrite the event completely.

This is how I rewrote my failure:

I told the boys to stay in the truck and got out. The driver rolled down his window and began yelling at me for almost hitting him.

I responded in a calm tone. I immediately apologized if he had thought I did something wrong by not giving way to him, and proceeded to tell him that it's a one-way street. I told him a story about another car doing the same thing to me last year, almost hitting us head on and causing severe harm to my family.

He apologized for not seeing the signs. I accepted and told him not to worry. Everyone makes mistakes. I asked him how the skiing was today. After he left, I proceeded to explain to Peter and his friends the lesson that could be learned from today's events.

The situation could have been 180 degrees different, but I know that I control my response to an event. It's one thing to practice and know how to unhook yourself from an emotion; it's another dimension to actually apply it to totally defuse the situation at hand. I am proud of myself for actually functionally applying my knowledge. I have the power to control my actions in the moment!

8 INVEST IN YOURSELF

Isn't it weird how we're inclined to put ourselves last all of the time? We put money into our car and our home, and call those our biggest investments. We take the car to the garage to get serviced regularly, and we never put diesel in a motor that takes gas. Yet, when it comes to our minds and our bodies, we're loath to make a financial commitment. We neglect them. We put crap in the tank all the time, choosing fast food over healthy, nourishing fuel. We don't make the time to exercise and keep everything strong and mobile. We don't schedule our maintenance, making sure there's enough time to rest up and let our parasympathetic system make all the necessary repairs. Then, when our bodies break down and collapse, we fork out grudgingly on health care, or cash in on insurance. Essentially, we treat the symptom instead of the real problem. We're surprised and annoyed that our bodies have failed us, when, truly, we've failed our bodies.

In reality, a little prevention and care *before* we experience trouble would go a long way to meaning we don't have to experience trouble at all. And some money spent willingly now could save a ton of heartache and even more money spent unwillingly later. Why wouldn't you protect your true vehicle – the body that carries you around and makes it possible to do anything? I think the same when it comes to your vision – why wouldn't you invest in it? In yourself? The returns you get from changing your reality are out of this world. Some money spent willingly now could mean a whole host of dividends appearing in the future.

It's amazing what you can achieve when you back yourself – if you overcome your reluctance and commit to what's important. Again, it's about prioritizing, but in this instance, I'm not just talking about your time, I'm talking about your money. If you have a clear vision of where you want to be, doing the math and investing in it is part of the surefire way to get there. This step is about putting your money where your mouth is, so to speak, and prioritizing your success over the day-to-day things you like to see in front of you and consider necessary. What could be more necessary than achieving your dreams?

YOUR GREATEST ASSET

You need to change your perspective when it comes to the way you view yourself. You are a vessel. You are a VIP. You are more valuable than any car or house or any other material thing. You're not just an asset – you are your greatest asset!

Investing in yourself is about admitting your self-worth. Your heart and mind are the intangible instruments that are going to imagine your vision and make it possible for you to get there. Your body is the tool that's going to take appropriate action along the way. Why wouldn't you nourish them?

You need to be able to stand in front of a mirror naked and accept yourself for who you are. Be comfortable in your own skin and really get to know yourself – focus on what makes you special and acknowledge what makes you great.

You are a champion! You have countless strengths and an infinite number of possibilities lie before you. Imagine investing in these strengths and enhancing your abilities.

This is about recognizing the worth within yourself so you can see it come to fruition all around you in the external world. You're the one who ascribes yourself value. You are your greatest asset.

FIND A MENTOR

The best thing I have ever done in every field that I have wanted to excel in has been to get myself a mentor.

Even back in college, when first starting out in strength and conditioning, I went and asked if I could learn from the head strength and conditioning coach at the University of Wyoming. I worked with the 6am athletes and soon learned it was the best thing I could have done to get practical experience towards my exercise sports science degree.

I did the same thing during my first internship after college. I was speaking with a person at the health club I was interning at and they told me about a strength coach, Mike Boyle, who was the Boston Bruins' strength coach at the time, running strength and conditioning camps for kids in Burlington, MA. After the conversation, I immediately drove to Boyle's Strength and Conditioning and asked where Mike was. I walked right up to him and told him my situation. I asked if I could intern for him. He said yes and the rest is history.

After that, I wanted to learn more, so I did a mentorship at the Institute for Human Performance in Boca-Rotan, Florida, under Juan Carlos Santana. He entirely changed the way I looked at strength and conditioning, and paved the way for all the successful work I did with clients in the years that followed.

In personal safety, I researched everyone I could find and through my studies I came across a gentleman named Tony Torres. I contacted him and flew him out so I could do multiple certifications with him. In terms of becoming an expert in personal safety, no one accelerated my progress more than Tony.

It was just when I needed a change in my life that I stumbled upon Brian Rose from London Real Academy. I saw an interview he conducted with a gentleman named Peter Sage, a renowned public speaker and expert in personal development. It blew my mind. I knew I had to contact Peter because he had what I wanted – a better understanding of life and how to live it on my terms. I contacted Peter's office and got the last spot in his first Elite Mentorship Forum, which changed my life.

Peter led me to one of his own mentors, the multi-billionaire entrepreneur Errol Abramson, who got me laser-focused on my passion. Errol has taught me a few things that will stick in my head for the rest of my life. I'll never forget him saying, "If I did it all over again, I would dream bigger!"

I was open to other opportunities that came thick and fast out of leftfield after that point. Meeting Scott Mann, an ex-Green Beret and leadership expert, was one such opportunity. I first heard of Scott from a friend I bumped into at a store! From the first mention of him, I knew I had to learn more and ended up speaking to him on the phone. I went on to enter his Pathfinder Mastermind/Coaching Program and haven't looked back. Scott has helped me become a better communicator and leader. He arrived at the exact time that I needed those skills in my life.

The moral of the story is that there is so much value to be unlocked through investing in yourself. Find a mentor, someone you want to model or learn from, and it will shorten your learning curve. Make sure you actually listen to them, take appropriate action, implement what they teach you and be proactive, no matter what it is that you do in life, and you will be amazed at what a catalyst they can be to your success.

Don't be afraid to invest in yourself. Don't be scared of a financial commitment. That will only help load the negative side of the scale and stop you from doing something that could change your life. On the other side of the coin, investing in yourself will boost your accountability and propel you toward your vision; it's only natural that you'll have more motivation to get the value out of something when you've ascribed value to it up front. And if you're motivated to get the value out of it, you'll get it!

Is there anyone in your current sphere of influence that you admire? This doesn't have to be someone you know personally – it could just be someone you've heard about and then researched. Are they achieving the kind of success you want make your reality? Or is there a specific thing they've done that you wish you knew how to implement in your own life?

Finding the right mentor might not actually involve any money – it might just be a commitment in terms of time and effort. There are so many people out there who are willing to help and generous with their time and expertise. So many people who've discovered a route to success, or learnt how to do something remarkable and are fired up to pass it on. Like I said in the beginning – it's not the kind of thing you keep to yourself! Sometimes, all you have to do is ask the question and you'll discover your greatest teacher.

You might not want to enter a formal mentorship program – perhaps you just want the answer to one burning question, or perhaps you want to speak with someone on a regular basis about what you're putting into practice, go over your progress and brainstorm next steps. My challenge to you is this: Find the person or people you feel could be the catalyst for your success, and just ask for a piece of their time. If the person's time has a price, or you identify a course you feel would be beneficial, then take the leap – invest in it. You'll be investing in your greatest asset – yourself.

9 COMMUNICATE WITH OTHERS

Communicating with others is how we connect with others. It is truly impossible to achieve success on your own. No one is an island. Whatever it is you want to do, other people will be involved somewhere. Even if your vision is to invent something entirely on your own, you're going to need to talk to people in order to obtain resources or even just to let people know about it so they can benefit from it when it's done.

Anything that ever happens begins with a conversation – whether that's a sale, an acquisition or simply the delivery of an idea. Communication is a powerful tool, and it can lead to incredible things.

It's equally important in your personal life as it is in your professional life, and is an integral factor in fulfilling relationships. You know the saying that a problem shared is a problem halved? I've found it to be more than true. The better I communicate with my wife, for example, the more amazing our marriage is. My wife Krissy has been with me on this journey for ten years, and we've truly grown into a team. It's really brought home to me how important it is to be with someone who supports you. Your partner is one of the closest people to you and, therefore, one of your biggest influences.

You choose your influences. And you choose how you communicate with others. It's one of the most important things you can work on when it comes to changing your reality. Connecting with others is rewarding in itself and can also mean giant leaps forward on the journey to your vision.

THE PRINCIPLE OF RECIPROCITY

When we have empathy for others, when we put ourselves in their shoes and understand what they're going through, that's when it's possible to connect with them.

Barbara Sher's TEDx talk *Isolation is the dream-killer, not your attitude* is a fantastic illustration of everything we're talking about in this step. She talks about going to these positive thinking seminars and being told to create your own reality, but she didn't really *believe* it was possible. Sher packed it in and then discovered reality really could be transformed when she started running encounter groups as a second job. She facilitated these gatherings where people would access their emotions and let it all out in order to work on their feelings.

One week, one of the members said his apartment was making him depressed, but he couldn't change it because he was depressed. The others saw this as fixable, and helped him get a new apartment. Much happier, he then decided he wanted a partner. Game for the challenge, the others helped him work on that as well, until he found someone.

Changing external reality wasn't supposed to be the focus of the group but it became the focus. Once everyone realized what they'd done for Ronnie had changed his world (bearing in mind that he had stood up and given them the opportunity to help), they understood that they could all pitch in and help change each other's worlds. As Sher says, "Amazing things started to happen."

What follows is success story after success story. Through it, Sher unfolded her own vision – to run a workshop and travel round the country teaching people how to be in these "success teams." At the end of the workshops, she'd say, "And now I'm going to prove it to you. Give me an impossible dream." People would offer them up *and then other people would make them come true*. From dancing with Patrick Swayze to running an animal refuge to becoming a ballerina at forty-four, Sher would get participants to name their wish and their obstacle ... and someone else in the crowd would always raise their hand, remove the obstacle and make it possible for their wish to be granted. As Sher shares delightedly, "You never know who you're talking to ... we are all the center of enormous amounts of information and connections that we don't need and we don't think of, unless somebody asks us."

Sher points out that we are problem-solving animals. If we gather a team around us and present them with a wish and an obstacle, people can't help themselves! They do it out of empathy and then amazing things happen for them as well, because of the principle of reciprocity.

We naturally want to help others, especially when, as is often the case, it's no skin off our nose! But then comes the kicker: When you're a helpful person, making connections and enabling things to happen for other people, people want to help you in return. It is reciprocity at work.

LEARN TO LISTEN

Someone told me to go watch that TEDx talk, and I'm so glad I listened to them. That proves my next point in itself! If we only listen, amazing things can come of it. Listen to that little voice in your gut, but also listen to other people. When you're open to new opportunities and ready to embrace whatever comes out of leftfield, then you'll notice things when they appear! So often, they'll crop up in conversations with other people. Other people can open the door to your dreams.

I already mentioned how I ended up meeting one of my greatest mentors, Scott Mann. I bumped into a friend at the store and he brought him up in the conversation – simple as that. The thing is if I hadn't been listening to him properly, I would have missed it. As it was, I heard what was said and was intrigued enough to follow up on it and learn more. The value that has come out of that first conversation has been incredible.

How do you make sure you don't miss anything? The secret is practicing "active listening."

When we talk to each other, we often aren't fully engaged in the conversation. Sometimes, we're only half attending to what's being said, more concerned with what *we're* going to say next and biding our time until we can be heard. There's even research that says we only remember twenty-five to fifty per cent of what we hear.

We do so many things without truly engaging, just going through the motions, and listening is one of them. Does that ring true for you? It's so easy to shut off, to disconnect from our environment and the people around us, and replace genuine connection with pseudo-engagement online. What we really need to be doing is having more conversations and really listening to the people around us.

There are several techniques that help you engage in active listening. Try to practice them every time someone talks to you.

ATTENDING BEHAVIORS

- Lean in, make eye contact and nod.
- Face your conversation partner fully and have an open posture.
- Don't fold your arms, turn your body away or constantly glance around to see what else is on offer.
- Don't get distracted. Even if you were meant to be focusing on another task and didn't

ask for this conversation, don't start thinking about other things you could be doing.

- Be present. Focus only on this conversation; ignore other conversations that might be happening around you.

OPEN-ENDED QUESTIONS

- Ask questions that keep the flow going and don't just require a yes/no answer, e.g. how do you feel about that?

SILENCE

- Be quiet when you're processing what is being said.
- Think about what the person speaking is saying, not about what you're going to say next.
- Don't interrupt. Let someone finish what they are saying before you comment on it or ask a question.

SUMMARIZING CONTENT AND REFLECTING FEELING

- Reflect back to them what the person is saying by paraphrasing part of it, summarizing their point, or asking a question to clarify what they mean.

Active listening is about truly paying attention. When we do, our attention is rewarded.

The next time you're in a conversation (and hopefully, every time you're in a conversation in the future!), make the conscious commitment to actively listen to the person you're speaking with.

Use your Quantum Success Journal to see what you remember when you listen actively, and make a note when something arises in conversation that you feel you ought to follow up and learn more about.

Assess your progress as well. Are you managing to put the techniques into practice every time you speak to someone, or are there certain times or circumstances when you find it really hard? Why is this? Can you work on it?

You can also track whether there's any change in your relationships as a result. If you found it difficult to communicate with people before, is it helping you connect? I've found that really paying attention to people and listening to what they have to say has been transformative, not only when it comes to individual interactions but also overall relationships.

10 CREATE YOUR REALITY

One Christmas, I bought Krissy a diamond key necklace. The key is such a powerful symbol. Things were really taking off in her business and I could see how incredible things were, and I wanted to give her something that represented it all – the key to success. And then something truly amazing happened to me while I was at the jewelry store. I looked in my wallet when it was time to pay for the necklace and found a piece of paper with a list of things written on it that I had envisioned for us six months before. I'd written them down and then let them go, turning my attention to taking appropriate action and trusting that life would meet us half way and we'd find ourselves where we wanted to be – I'd forgotten all about the piece of paper.

When I read what I had written, I cried. As of the day before, we had hit every single thing I'd put down on paper! Instead of a Christmas card, along with the necklace, I gave Krissy the old, scribbled note.

Nothing could show more clearly that we are the creators of our destiny. The actions we take every day make our dreams and visions come true.

We create our own reality and the universe delivers! When you believe in something down to your core and take action, it will happen for you. It simply has to happen. Your body can't exist in a world that it wasn't meant for; the universe will open its doors for you. Life is truly amazing!

Too many people focus on the negatives instead of focusing on the positives. My default program is now one of positive thinking, and I want it to be yours as well. When your inner world is filled to the brim with positive thoughts and intentions, they can't help but overflow into your external reality. Like attracts like. You get what you ask for – that's what you deserve.

BELIEVE IN YOURSELF

I want to talk about one of my mentees here, Nick, who's got all the success in the world ahead of him. He's a case study, in a way, showing that putting all of this guidance into practice can truly mean change. If you don't already take my word and everything I've been through as proof of what's possible, then take his story as an example of how you can turn your reality around 180 degrees.

Nick and I actually met through our kids playing soccer. His career had always been in manufacturing. When we started working together, he was an inventory analyst for a local company.

What became very obvious very quickly was that in reality, he's an entrepreneur. Talking about my influences and what I'd done with my life, and the chance that *everyone* has to change their life, resonated with Nick strongly, though he'll tell you that, at first, he thought I was kind of crazy! It took a while for the message to sink in, but then, as he says, he started taking chances.

He'd created a safe, comfortable life for his family, and never taken huge risks. With his change in perspective, only last year, Nick went out on a limb and started an e-commerce business. As he says, he was "still not taking huge risks, but taking the right risks." It had to be built from scratch, with no prior experience to lean on. But because of his approach, things quickly got out of control – in a good way! Now he's built his own software and is in the midst of marketing it. He knew he was a creator – he just had to access this whole new vision for his life in order to take the appropriate action to make it a reality.

Nick was surrounded by people with good jobs, committed to a certain mode of life, but he wanted more. He just needed someone to ask him, "What are you doing? Why are you settling?" That's confronting to begin with and more than challenging. It's even unwelcome – it can make you uncomfortable. But, as he says, it made more and more sense. Nick was able to distance himself from people with negative energy and brought his inner circle, who supported his vision, tighter and closer. Then life really started to change.

What he had to deal with in terms of challenge was a whole lot of conditioning that had come before and that sometimes held him back from taking bold actions without seeking external validation first. He *knew* what the right moves were; he could feel it. His gut was on his side and his ideas were spot on, but his self-belief was shaky in the beginning – the proof wasn't there before him yet, so doubt would try to rear its head, especially when the roadblocks hit.

At one point, Nick was attacked by competitors on Amazon. He got notice just before the fourth quarter, just before Thanksgiving, that he had violated a copyright infringement that he had no clue about. He actually hadn't – it was a tactic to put him out of business. A competitor had made an underhand claim and he was at risk of losing his account.

Nick admits that he thought about saying, "Okay, I'm done. This is too much. I've put too much money into this and it's going to fail." He had the option of staying comfortable, staying in the status quo, and sticking with his former life when things got scary. But he didn't give in to it. He changed his attitude to seeing his roadblocks as learning experiences, and because he was able to do that, he overcame them. He was able to tell himself that everything was going to be fine. Now, things like that don't even matter! It was temporary. Your current state is temporary.

Now, he says, he realizes it's all about your perception of reality. "Everybody is living in this dream that you have full control over… It is just a choice."

Attitude is everything. That's why it's so important to have the right kind of support around you. The wrong, negative influences whispering in your ear can quickly kill your dreams if you're already half inclined to agree with them. You need a mentor or a team you can go to who will give you that push because they see your potential. The more they, and you, are proved right, the easier it is to believe in yourself.

Nick will tell you how easy it is to hit a snag or roadblock and start talking yourself out of things. If anything's difficult, most people will haul themselves out of it. Learning how to overcome that is life-changing. Turning roadblocks into learning experiences – actually putting that into practice – isn't an easy thing.

I could tell from the get-go that this guy could do anything. Inside, he knew it too. And we were both right! He's working hard and kicking butt, and getting everything he deserves. He's hungry, he's driven, he's constantly looking for new opportunities – and that approach gets rewarded.

Nick describes it as a perfect storm. He started pushing outside his comfort zone in one area of his life, and it made it easier to do so in other areas. He met me at that time – exactly the right time. He'd never played soccer but managed to score a spot on a team. He says the first time he went out on the field he was insanely nervous. What was he doing out there? He didn't know what the heck he was doing and felt like a fool. He describes feeling foolish as a powerful emotion – it can so easily stop someone from doing something. He didn't want to stick with it, but he did. After a pep talk or two, he adjusted his attitude. He went out there to play hard, even though, in the beginning, he hated his Sundays. And by the end of the season, he was a starting player.

Now, looking back, Nick connects the dots and sees the parallels in the different areas of his life. Acting on his ideas is now guaranteed. Success is assured.

Just believe in yourself and that kind of change can be yours. It's already in your hands!

SEE LIFE AS A REFLECTION

It was one of my mentors who first taught me to look at life as a reflection. This piece of wisdom was life changing for me. Once I really got it, that's when creating my reality became possible. Once I understood that the outside, physical world is a reflection of the inner, metaphysical world, I understood that everything was possible – because I control my inner state! I'm the captain of my ship, in charge of my heart and mind. I'm the one who steers the course and that means I'm the one who's responsible for the reflection that stares back at me.

What can be challenging, when you first understand, accept and attempt to apply the concept, is the delay that can be part of the process. Sometimes, the effects can be pretty immediate – just wake up and decide to improve everyone else's day with a smile. Be genuinely interested in people, offer a small token of kindness, and see the response you receive right away. However, concrete change often doesn't happen overnight. You can align your heart and mind with where you want to be, and start living *as if when without*, but to begin with, you're still without. What you see in your external world can come from the inner reality you were broadcasting weeks ago – you've always had the power to create your physical world, and the one you're currently living in is the byproduct of that. You've attracted what you've most asked for. Even if you want something very badly, and feel as though you've asked the universe for it, you can cancel the order, so to speak, with your secret but strong belief that you're not *really* ever going to get it. You might think you're doing everything right, but your belief system has to be aligned with your thoughts and actions. You must not be impatient; you must not see the time delay as a sign that you're never going to receive what you want.

It's so hard to overcome this! In this age of instant gratification, we all want everything right *now*. We're used to getting things straight away. But while that's good motivation to understand that right now is the time to act, as well as cultivating our vision, we have to cultivate patience. Perhaps it's easiest to understand with a very physical example. Say you go to the gym and work out for the first time. You don't ask life for the strength to pick up the heavier weights right away. You just wouldn't expect to be able to, and you'd be right! Instead, you train, usually for three to five weeks, before you build up your basic strength. You progress through different phases on the journey: conditioning, hypertrophy, strength, power and power endurance. Each phase has a specific repetition range to adhere to in your workouts. You commit to the process and do what you need to do over and over.

Neural adaptation takes place when your nervous system adapts to a new movement pattern and other processes, such as recovery. Your body adapts to the stress you place on it in each workout. This whole process allows you to use heavier weights down the road.

You know exactly what you're aiming for and exactly what to do to get there. In the mental gym, you're already there. But there is a delay in the physical gym. There is a delay in the mirror, where you look at your external reflection. Results take time; you can't force them or try to rush them. You can't try to change, in an instant something, which has already been created. There are processes that have to happen before you get what you are looking for.

If you want your outer world to change, you must look internally and focus on your metaphysical world before the physical world can give you what you want. But you must let go of impatience. You can't constantly narrow your eyes at the universe and demand to know *when* and *how* and, worst of all, *now!* Such behavior displays your doubt, and your doubt will be reflected back at you.

You have to trust. Things will change, little by little, and then, radically, everything will be different. Like when you work on your weight, fitness and muscle tone – at first, you may not see the physical change. If you look in the mirror every day, the subtleties will be hard to spot. But if you don't obsess about staring in the mirror – say you avoid looking for the signs for a few weeks – suddenly, you'll notice a change. It'll be obvious! It'll be so obvious, other people will point it out to you!

Expect a delay and let go of the details. Don't look for an immediate shift. Take what comes and trust. Once you change the state of your inner world, mentally and emotionally, the outer world has to change accordingly, to balance out the new you.

When you think about this balancing act, think about it in terms of bank accounts. I'm sure you know someone who's always chasing the dollar. They live for their paycheck and are always hemming and hawing over these get-rich-quick schemes. They're the epitome of the people who demand satisfaction now. These are the people who talk constantly about money. They are never happy with what they have; they say they never have enough. And if they do get their hands on some windfall, something bad happens and they lose it. That or it all immediately disappears on credit cards and bills that they've been racking up, and they feel like they never had it in the first place.

Too many people connect their emotional bank account to their financial bank account! Not only are they doing it backwards, they are sabotaging themselves. They are constantly trying to create wealth, but they see wealth as this external event. They perceive it to be the cause of happiness and a necessary condition for feelings of abundance. They don't realize that, in truth, the only way to get what you want financially is to create an inner world of abundance first.

You must separate your emotional bank account from your physical bank account. You must have an emotional bank account stocked high with abundance in order to take action, create more opportunities for yourself and attract wealth in the external world, bringing your accounts into balance. The wealth isn't the cause of your happiness and abundance; *you* are the cause of your happiness and abundance. The wealth is the effect you produce.

These external effects are the reflection of your inner state. They are what you cause to come into being. You are all-powerful! And if you are all-powerful, you can be all-patient as well. Don't worry about the delay in the reflection changing. Worry and fear foster more worry and fear. Stay present and focused, and the picture will change. You are constantly causing ripples that alter your reality.

PRACTICE GRATITUDE

Above, I mentioned the people who are never happy with what they've got. What they don't get is that the more grateful you are, the more you get! But I'm not talking about paying lip service here. Like with everything I've mentioned throughout this book, you have to truly feel the emotion. Consider all the reasons you have to be grateful and engage your heart alongside your mind. Feel it. There is no tricking the universe. Genuine feelings of gratitude are what grant you further reasons to be grateful.

Be grateful for others' success! Errol always says, "Your success is my reward." I know exactly what he means. When you are grateful for others' success, it's your success, because we are all one. Success attracts more success.

It can take work to train your brain to be positive and it can take work to train your heart to be grateful. It's about stepping out of a victim mentality, where you perceive bad things are always happening to you, and a scarcity mentality, where you perceive that you don't have anything or ever get given anything, and believing yourself to be blessed, as you are. There are so many things to be grateful for! Rather than bemoaning what you lack, you should be celebrating everything you have and everything to come.

I am so grateful for every single thing that has happened to me, even the bad stuff. Sometimes the greatest abundance comes out of the darkest shadows. It can be hard to feel grateful when things are bleak. That's why it's so important to believe that things will get better. You have to envision a time when everything makes sense. You have to be grateful that you're going to bring it into being.

exercise: Express Your Gratitude

This exercise is twofold. As well as expressing gratitude in private, being thankful for everything great in your life and everything great to come, I want you to express your gratitude more when it comes to the others around you. Think about how you feel when someone gives thanks for something you've done. You feel recognized and appreciated. You feel like you have done something that matters and made a difference. Too often, we can let please and thank you slide, but they are so important. They show respect as well as gratitude, and they can make someone's day.

Sometimes, there is nothing so powerful as showing some appreciation. As a friend of mine recently commented, "I must say, there is magic in the words thank you." From the act of thanking the bus driver when you get off at your stop to thanking that significant person in your life who stood by you when things were toughest, express your gratitude. We wouldn't get anywhere without each other! So say thank you when it's warranted. It might mean simply saying those two words, or it might mean putting in the effort to show someone what their actions really meant to you. Regardless, give gratitude when it's due. Put it into practice every day at every opportunity.

As usual, I also want you to write it down. Record what you're grateful for each day. You can do this in a separate gratitude journal or simply include it in your Quantum Success Journal. It is part and parcel of your quest to change your reality – appreciate it! Be thankful for your vision, for where you're going to be, but be thankful for where you are now as well. Without this point, you wouldn't get where you're going.

- Write down three to five things you are grateful for each day. They can be things that have happened, things that are happening, people in your life, even people no longer in your life!

- Revisit your list, day on day, and add items as you go.
- Don't rush this and scribble things down for the sake of it. Stop and think; engage your heart and mind. Reflect on why you are grateful and let the feelings flow through your whole body and mind.

Here are some examples from my own gratitude journal:

- I am grateful for being able to change the world
- I am grateful for being the cause
- I am grateful for saying YES!
- I am grateful for being interested
- I am grateful for being an influencer
- I am grateful for attraction
- I am grateful for helping people
- I am grateful for my wife and her unconditional love
- I am grateful for my children's love
- I am grateful for knowing reality is subject to influence!

FORGE THE KEY TO SUCCESS

I hope you've gathered by now that, unlike the necklace that I gave to my wife, you don't just get gifted the key to success.

It's like Jim Carrey said on Oprah in 1997, "You can't just visualize and you know, go eat a sandwich."

Jim Carrey's a great example of how to put visualization into practice. When he was broke, he used to drive to the most affluent areas and really smell the leather, so to speak. He had nothing, but he'd envision directors being interested in him and confirm to himself that the things he wanted were out there. He even wrote himself a check for ten million dollars for acting services rendered, dating it Thanksgiving 1995. He kept it in his wallet, where it deteriorated, but skip ahead to Thanksgiving '95 and that piece of paper proved its value. He discovered he was going to make ten million dollars with *Dumb and Dumber.* As Oprah responds to his story, "Visualization works if you work hard!"

But harnessing the power of your intention, realizing that you are a creator of reality and able to bring things into existence, is also fun! Carrey is the first to say it, and it resonates with a line from his movie *Yes Man*, which I mentioned before. In the movie, Allison (Zooey Deschanel), the girl who came out of leftfield when Carrey's character, Carl, started saying "yes" to opportunities that came his way, describes her incredibly free approach to life. She does what she loves, and she enjoys every moment of it. "The world's a playground," she says at one point. "You know that when you're a kid, but somewhere along the way, everyone forgets it."

Don't forget it! Remember what it was like to be a kid? Remember when someone asked you what you wanted to be? We may have been conditioned to grow up and stop acting like a child who has faith that everything they ever want can be theirs, but it's a choice to take the step back into that mindset!

Everything you want *can* be yours. You need to envision it, engage your emotions and forge the key to success. Creating the key is about taking appropriate action. Just make sure you enjoy it at the same time! Enter into things with a relentless work ethic and passion for what you are doing.

How do you get passion? That's simple – follow your heart. When you do that, you will tap into an energy source that will catapult you past the moon and stars. When you do something you love, you can put unlimited time and energy into it without even noticing. Trust me, my wife used to do the corporate thing, working nine to five, making money for someone else and not enjoying it, and now she works for herself. She couldn't be happier and she's crushing it!

In his 2014 commencement speech at the Maharishi University of Management, Jim Carrey talked about his dad, whom he says could have been the most brilliant comedian, but who didn't take a chance on it because he didn't believe it was possible for him. He made the conservative choice and got a safe job as an accountant instead, but then, when Carrey was twelve, he got let go from his job and the family had to do whatever they could to survive. Carrey says he learnt many great lessons from his father ... "not the least of which was that you can fail at what you don't want, so you might as well take a chance on doing what you love."

If you don't take action, life can't respond to you. The universe can't help you get to where you want to be. Instead, you will just react to whatever life throws your way. That's living in an "effect" state rather than a "cause" state. That's getting out of bed each morning and thinking you have to face the day, rather than believing that you can create the day.

You know that feeling you get on Christmas morning? You're off work and you're going to spend the day with your loved ones. Everyone's going to be giving and receiving gifts. The kids are going to be so excited and you're going to eat the treats that come at Christmas along with all the trimmings – with no guilt! You're excited and feeling the buzz of anticipation. You know, without a doubt, that it's going to be this amazing day!

Every single day can be like this. It's not the external event (Christmas) that causes the feelings – it's you! You can choose to feel that way every day. You can choose to wake up in the morning and heave a sigh, think of five negative things before breakfast, drag your feet and let every challenging encounter ruin your day. Or you can wake up in the morning with a bright outlook, think of five positive things that are going to come your way, enjoy every mouthful of your breakfast, and face whatever challenges the day holds with a spring in your step.

There's another movie I want to mention here called *About Time*. In it, the main character, Tim, played by Domhnall Gleeson, finds out from his father that the men in their family can time-travel. Light-hearted adventures ensue, with Tim using the power to help him capture Mary, the love of his life, played by Rachel McAdams, but there's a deep, heartfelt message underneath it all. Though he makes the attempt, Tim can't stop life from having its ups and downs, and, come the end, he realizes that he shouldn't try to.

When Tim's father (Bill Nighy) sits him down and asks, "Do you want to know the big secret, or would you rather find it out for yourself like I did?" he responds, understandably, with, "Go on, tell me. Let's save some time."

Tim then shares this secret – "the mothership" – with us.

And so he told me his secret formula for happiness.

Part one of the two-part plan was that I should just get on with ordinary life, living it day by day, like anyone else.

But then came part two of dad's plan. He told me to live every day again. Almost exactly the same. The first time with all the tensions and worries that stop us noticing how sweet the world can be, but the second time ... noticing.

We get to see the difference between one day and the "next." And the difference lies not just in Tim's own attitude but in the people around him. You see the smiles he elicits in response to his second-day demeanor. You see the way he helps people take things less seriously. You can imagine them passing that on, rather than transmitting more doom and gloom to the others they come into contact with.

Think about what happens when you have a rough day at work and you take the bad feelings away with you. You come home and what happens? You probably get into an argument with your spouse, who could be have been having a great day, but you ruin it, because yours was ruined. Because you have chaos in your inner world, you create chaos in your outer world. It just doesn't have to be that way – you control your inner world.

Come the end of *About Time*, Tim has figured out his own approach, his own big secret to happiness.

The truth is, I now don't travel back at all. Not even for the day. I just try to live every day as if I've deliberately come back to this one day. To enjoy it. As if it was the full, final day of my extraordinary, ordinary life.

We're all travelling through time together. Every day of our lives. All we can do is do our best to relish this remarkable ride.

You and I don't have the ability to time-travel, so it should be an even easier decision to make. Rather than going through life wishing you could alter things, *create them*. Cause the world to respond to your actions and, I promise, your life will change. That's the true key to success.

Take out your journal and reread what you've written about your vision so far. Look at the picture again if you've drawn it out. This reality is in your grasp!

Now think. What is one thing you need to do to commit to it? What's the biggest step between here and there – the boldest move? What scares you about taking it?

Is it investing some money? Quitting your day job? Leaving home? Removing yourself from the influence of someone toxic? These are not small things. They are radical.

Visualize yourself taking the step. Now, you've already taken it. What's the worst that has happened? What's the best that has happened? Write the answers down in your journal. Really get into the details.

Imagine the best possible outcome and place yourself in that picture. From that place of success, look back at the moment when you had to make your radical decision and consider whether it was worth it. Are you glad you took that step despite all the fear and uncertainty around it?

Remember, success is a certainty if you believe it is.

Now, just imagine, for the sake of argument that ten challenges arose in the period between. It turned out you had to navigate stormy waters with some devastating waves, like Steve Jobs when he was fired from Apple, or me eleven years ago. But you came through it all, and you made it to the shore of success. It's everything you ever dreamed it would be. Now you're here, bumps behind you, looking back, would you *still* make that decision? Chances are, you wouldn't change a thing. Despite what happened when he was thirty, Steve Jobs would still have chosen to start Apple in his garage at twenty. And now I'm here, I can connect the dots as well. And it was all worth it.

If you need to take a radical step and just physically can't do it right away, write down your intention to do it. Even put a date on it, like Jim Carrey's check.

Faith is the most powerful force there is. It moves mountains. Believe in yourself and take that leap of faith.

CONCLUSION

If Richard Branson were born with your life, with all your circumstances and challenges, do you think he'd still make himself a billionaire? If you've been paying attention, I think you'll have realized by now that the answer is a resounding yes.

Does that sound a bit crazy? Good! I think Steve Jobs put it best when he said, "The ones who are crazy enough to think they can change the world are the ones who do!"

There's been a lot of information in this book, but the last thing you should feel is overwhelmed. If you haven't started already, the best way to get going is to begin with the exercises found in each chapter. Making the time to work on the exercises can be the first of all the positive habits you cultivate. Forming positive habits and changing things little by little is the key to achieving your ultimate vision.

FORM POSITIVE HABITS

The key to altering your inner, metaphysical world, and, therefore, your external reality, is taking little, positive steps daily. This is what creates positive habits. It's important to live in the moment and not put too much pressure and stress on yourself by demanding giant leaps where little steps will mean long-lasting change.

I love the people who tell me they don't have the time; they are too busy, they wish they could but can't right now – maybe down the road. Sound familiar? Trust me – I've heard it all.

We all have the same twenty-four hours in a day. It's what we choose to do with those twenty-four hours that will make the difference when it comes to where we get on our journey. At the end of the day, that's what makes us all different.

You have the ability to choose where you want to be in life – it's your life. Most choose the path of least resistance and being comfortable. Instead, try getting *un*comfortable!

Do you have time for TV, movies, the news, the Internet, texting, social media or talking on your phone? Think about all the things you make time for in your day without thinking about it. These are habits that you have engraved in your mind over many days, months and years. Facebook, anyone?

When it comes to the habits you create, whether negative or positive, they are formed the same way. When we are moving forward with a positive or negative habit, there is not a lot of difference in behavior. In the beginning, there's not much of an effect from either.

For example, if you work out once, it's not going to get you fit – just sore, right? Going to KFC one time isn't going to make you fat, correct?

But after about three weeks or so, you start to see a substantial change happening. You are building a neural pathway in your brain for whatever activity you are doing, whether it's mental, physical or spiritual. The first time is naturally the hardest with any new activity, but it's a heck of a lot easier after a few weeks.

Let's take me, for example. I started to take ice-cold showers, probably a year-and-a-half ago, for the mental and physical benefits. In the beginning, my mind would tell me not to do it, and before I even got in the cold water, I would be shivering. It was tough, but I kept doing it anyway. I kept telling my mind to "shut up" and I would get in. Now, I can't stand hot showers. I actually enjoy the cold. I feel so much better afterwards. I'm more relaxed and my sleep is amazing. Imagine if I had listened to my logical brain telling me not to do it – I would be in the same place as I was eighteen months ago. You *have* to get uncomfortable to move forward in life.

It usually takes about thirty days to develop a new habit. This means you can make a new habit every thirty days, which creates twelve new habits in a year, which can change your life because your behavior has now changed. Who you become over the span of twelve months is now the new you.

By this point your identity has changed! This is what reprogramming your mind is all about. Without changing your identity, you will never change anything in your life.

So, with all this in mind, here are some ways you can take small steps each day to form ten positive habits in terms of your personal development. This is all part of your Quantum Success Plan!

1. **Take responsibility** – Write down your declaration of accountability: *I take responsibility for my reality*. Write it in your Quantum Success Journal and/or on a Post-it that you stick to your mirror. Wherever it is, re-read it every single day. Make it the first thing you think, say and *believe* each morning.

2. **Access your vision** – Make sure you've written down, drawn and/or made a mind movie of your ultimate vision. Revisit this every day as well, in your mind. Your vision should be your overwhelming concern, so hold it in your head as well as on a page somewhere. Remember, you can add to or alter the picture as new opportunities and developments arise. The key is to let go of goals. Don't get bogged down with exactly how and when it's going to happen. Just let your vision unfold.

3. **Trust your gut** – Every day, whenever you're faced with a decision, consult your intuition. If you find yourself engaging your brain and arguing your right to fail, take a breath, and align your heart and mind. Ask your inner self what to do and follow your gut.

4. **Design your environment** – Detox in all three aspects of your environment – places, people and media. Every single day, make a small choice for the better, whether it's to de-clutter your desk, refuse an invitation to have your ear chewed off by a Debbie downer, or ban your cell phone from the bedroom.

5. **Look after yourself** – Begin keeping your health and wellness journal. This is as simple as carrying a small pad of paper or making a note on your calendar. Record your nutrition, exercise and recovery habits for thirty days, and, each day, circle anything that's not to your benefit. Reduce the number of circles week-by-week, day-by-day.

6. **Break down your barriers** – Write down your positive affirmations and practice them every day. Repeat them to yourself before you go to sleep at night and when you wake up in the morning, and engage your emotions. These affirmations embody your reality.

7. **Reframe failure** – Day by day, refuse to focus on your failures in a negative way. Record anything that goes wrong as a bump in the road to achieving your vision – one that you learn from and therefore helps you excel. Don't fear failure; embrace it! This will become easier every time you see the benefit unfold, but believe in the benefit before you see it.

8. **Invest in yourself** – Practice looking in the mirror each day and recognizing that what stares back at you is your most valuable asset! Every day, do something to invest in yourself and improve yourself, whether it's buying a book, reading an article, watching a TED talk, committing to a course, or just asking a question of someone you know could help you.

9. **Communicate with others** – In every conversation you have, big or small, practice active listening. Really engage with the person speaking and pay attention. Focus on being interested in others! Don't only do it when you think the conversation is important; every conversation is important. Don't only do it with people you know; you never know who you're talking to.

10. **Create your reality** – Every single morning, wake up and, quite simply, tell yourself what an amazing day it is. Get up and choose to feel like it's Christmas morning. Put a spring in your step – great things are going to happen; they are already happening! Be grateful for everything that is, and everything the day has in store. Thank everyone who does you a service, big or small. Every day, every act, brings you closer to your vision.

Forming each habit begins with the mind. Every single action you take starts with a decision. The first secret to stopping doing something is questioning yourself and realizing you are doing it. Each day, consciously assess how you behave and decide how you want to behave. That's when you can begin to stop one behavior and cultivate another.

What comes next? That's up to you! Just remember, practice makes permanence. Please keep this book as your personal development bible and go back over the ideas and exercises to reinforce the beliefs and hone the practices that will get you everything you dream of.

The revolution is here. Come join ReWiredAcademy.com, a brotherhood of new leaders living a life of impact, wealth and freedom giving you the help and support you need every step of the way to live the way you were meant to live.

I'd wish you good luck, but you don't need it! Everything is possible. Just believe that and believe in yourself. Remember: Everything begins with a thought. Taking appropriate action transforms that thought into your reality!

APPENDIX
60 Quantum Tips

1. Celebrate often
2. Smile
3. Be humble & grateful
4. Have fun
5. Dream, Imagine, Act
6. Have a vision bigger than you
7. Be interested, not interesting
8. Take appropriate action
9. Make yourself uncomfortable
10. Be limitless
11. Follow your passion
12. Surround yourself with who you want to become
13. Turn off technology
14. Find a mentor

15. Never put anyone on a pedestal
16. Be in the moment
17. Understand the power of your story
18. Breathe deep and focus
19. Do it!
20. Have a vision that people call crazy
21. Keep moving
22. Find your spark
23. Eat healthy and rest up
24. Challenge your preconceived notions of the world
25. Explore new things
26. Leave your tracks
27. Say thank you ... express gratitude.
28. Don't be afraid to fail
29. Find balance
30. Have humility
31. Don't overthink things: KISS (keep it simple, stupid!)
32. Don't be afraid to ask for help
33. Have conversations
34. Be hungry and never settle
35. Don't obsess over the good opinion of others (GOOP)
36. Write things down
37. Give back

38. Get up early
39. Lead by example
40. Work hard
41. Put yourself first
42. Stay grounded
43. Listen to your gut
44. Align your heart and mind
45. Drop the dead wood
46. Adopt positive habits
47. Play
48. Drink lots of water
49. Flow with the current
50. Be authentic
51. Listen
52. Love unconditionally
53. Believe in yourself
54. Practice what you preach
55. Learn to forgive
56. Regimen, Ritual, Rigor
57. Don't complain
58. Be empathetic
59. Put yourself out there
60. Follow your passion

BIBLIOGRAPHY

Byrne, Rhonda (2006) *The Secret,* Dharma Production (http://www.thesecret.tv/products/the-secret-film-download/)

Campbell, Tom (2017) "My Big TOE" (www.my-big-toe.com)

Carrey, Jim (2014) MUM Commencement Address, Maharishi University of Management (http://news.stanford.edu/2005/06/14/jobs-061505/)

Dubrowolski, Patti (2012) "Draw your future", TEDx Rainier (https://tedxseattle.com/talks/draw-your-future/)

Forbes, Kent (2015) *The Simulation Hypothesis,* Fair Wind Films (http://www.fairwindfilms.com/store/p1/The_Simulation_Hypothesis.html)

Hill, Napoleon (1937) *Think and Grow Rich*, The Ralston Society

Jobs, Steve (2005) Stanford Commencement Address, Stanford University (http://news.stanford.edu/2005/06/14/jobs-061505/)

McKernan, Phillip (2014) *Rich on Paper, Poor on Life*, Braveheart Media

Mod, Craig (2017) "How I Got My Attention Back", Backchannel.com

Newman, James (1977) *Release Your Brakes*, Pace Organization

Newport, Cal (2016) 'Quit Social Media', TEDx Tysons (http://tedxtysons.com/)

Pausch, Randy (2007)) "Really Achieving Your Childhood Dreams" ("The Last Lecture"), Carnegie Mellon University (https://www.ted.com/talks/randy_pausch_really_achieving_your_childhood_dreams)

Pena, Daniel (1999) *Your First 100 Million*, Medina

Sher, Barbara (2015) "Isolation is the dream-killer, not your attitude", TEDx Prague (http://www.tedxprague.cz/en/videa/isolation-is-the-dream-killer-not-your-attitude-barbara-sher)

Wattles, Wallace (1910) *The Science of Getting Rich*, Elizabeth Towne Company

ACKNOWLEDGEMENTS

First and foremost I want to thank my wife Kristina for supporting me even when it looked like nothing but a huge dream, we made it and I couldn't have attained it without your love and support. We are both doing exactly what we are supposed to be doing with our lives right now and it is amazing what we can accomplish together as a team.

Thank you to my children who have given me the opportunity to be the best dad and person I can be every day. Walking you to the bus, playing tag, tubing, surfing, hanging out on the boat, driving you to school and every other little thing we do are touch points in my life that I will never forget. That is what life is about, little moments that last a lifetime. As parents we wanted to show you that everything is possible when you believe in yourself, have a vision bigger than you and help people by providing tremendous value. You must grow and contribute every day and not be afraid to get uncomfortable. When things look down, take action, get creative and I promise, it will all work out. Never stop moving! Dreams do come true, they may take a long time to manifest but they do become a reality, your reality! All it takes is a thought followed by appropriate action!

To the, "Winners" Lance, Chris, Sean & Nick who have supported me and pushed me to go after it relentlessly, who believe in me and my vision just as much as I do, you guys are truly limitless and I can't thank you enough.

We are never done learning and when the student is ready for the teacher he or she may appear. When you truly discover whom you are deep down in your core you will start living the way you were meant to live.

I have had the honor and privilege of working with, learning from and researching some of the top strength and conditioning coaches, personal safety instructors as well as personal development and leadership coaches in the world.

I would like to thank my personal development mentors for teaching me that my outer world is truly a reflection of my inner world and truly helping me see that everything is possible, that we truly are limitless and everything happens with a delay. A new future really is available right now. When my mindset changed, our lives changed!

In addition, I would like to give a special thanks to my mentor Scott Mann for helping me become a better communicator through connection and story. You opened my eyes to a whole new world when it comes to communicating, influencing and leading without a title.

To my fellow Spartan's, leave your tracks, go after it with everything you have to create the world that does not yet exist and make it your reality right now! When you have a vision that is bigger than you, everything is possible!

There are way too many to list on this page but this book is a result of everything I have learned from the people I have worked with and the people I have researched. I owe all the mentors, teachers and coaches who have ever helped me in any way a big thank you!

In addition I would like to thank my editors from Grammar Factory, Jacqui, Carolyn and especially Sara, without you, this doesn't happen! I also want to thank my team at Morgan James Publishing who gave me a chance to prove myself again, thank you!

ABOUT THE AUTHOR

Matt Tamas is a high-performance leadership coach and the founder of ReWiredAcademy.com. His calling is to bring together likeminded men who want to lead a life of impact, wealth and freedom; to give them the tools and support they need to live the life they were meant to live.

www.TheMorganJamesSpeakersGroup.com

We connect Morgan James published authors with live and online events and audiences who will benefit from their expertise.

Printed in the USA
CPSIA information can be obtained
at www.ICGtesting.com
JSHW082344140824
68134JS00020B/1869

9 781683 506034